14 – 18

THE FINAL WORD
FROM THE TRENCHES OF THE
FIRST WORLD WAR

First Published 1993
2nd Edition - revised and enlarged with extra interviews 2003
3rd Edition 2018
Published by Stagedoor Publishing
London WC1N 3XX UK

www.zoism.co.uk

My Thanks

to so many individuals and organisations who gave
their advice and time to help me as I worked on this book.
Above all I thank them for caring about 1914–18.

My wife, Patricia, who came to most of
the interviews and helped to 'break the ice' and to:

George Hall
Lee Ferro
Janet Seignior
Rita Hind
The Western Front Association
The Royal British Legion
The Salvation Army
The British Red Cross Association
The Daily Mail
The Church Army

Stagedoor Publishing – Who had the courage to publish when
others said 'we like it but it's too risky and not *PC*'

This book is dedicated
to the millions who spent
the remainder of their lives
grieving for that special someone
who never came home

Contents

Foreword

As each day we slip further into the future, very soon the 1914–18 War will be beyond living memory. It will be part of that huge dream we call the past. It will be as far away as The Battles of Trafalgar or Waterloo, and as obscure as the Battle of Hastings in 1066. Anything written then about the years 1914–18 will be pure conjecture and second-hand guess work, probably well informed and carefully researched, but still the work of people who were not even born until decades after the event and who will unconsciously put their own slant or personal interpretation on those years and times. In fact, so much for truthful history.

This book, dear reader, is then unique because it's a last look at that War, fought by men now near the end of their long lives, who were there. They are talking with the perspective that time always brings. But they are speaking from the heart. The usual war book written by military historians can tell you the exact time a battle started and the correct reason we won or lost that battle but they cannot tell you about being petrified, cold, wet and starving, or indeed, desperately homesick. But the men you are about to meet can and do tell of those things. I have written their stories exactly as they were told to me, in their own words. If they made a grammatical mistake then it's been left in. I was shocked and saddened by what these foot soldiers told me of their conditions and suffering. I grew up in the air raids of the 1939–45 War, and later was in the Army myself. But even this experience of war and army life could never equip me to write with any real insight into what they called 'The Great War'. I travelled far and wide to meet these men, all of them between ninety and one-hundred and four years old. I interviewed well over twice this number but their story will not appear in this book. Sadly, old age had taken its toll. Many were too deaf to conduct a proper interview. In others the memory was now too unreliable and times, dates and places had all become blurred. Therefore, the men in this book are like rare gems. They were all in good mental shape and could hold what was at times spellbinding conversation. Their tale has a constant theme of extreme hardship, in every way, fear of being killed, not months but years spent in cold, wet rat-infested filthy conditions. Constant hunger and thirst, and the unburied dead for company. These recollections are living proof of how much the human spirit can endure and still come through with dignity.

As I look back on my meetings with these men I realise they all had something in common. They did not know each other and they came from different walks of life. Was it a certain style? So many words come to mind but one word that can describe them all is integrity. That's the impression I am left with after getting to know these last few remaining survivors. It's the last time they will talk to anyone face to face about their part in one of the world's greatest tragedies. I feel proud that they were willing to share their experiences with me so that, long after they and us have left the battlefield, others yet to come will know what it was like to be there in 1914–18.

Terry Cunningham
London, 2003

World War I

From August 4th 1914

To

November 11th 1918

Was a war between what were known as the **Allied Powers** and the **Central Powers**.

The **Allied Powers** were Great Britain and the British Empire, France, Russia, Belgium, Japan and Serbia and from May 1915 Italy; March 1916 Portugal; April 1917 U.S.A; July 1917 Greece; August 1917 China.

The **Central Powers** were Germany, Austria, Hungary and from November 1914 Turkey; October 1915 Bulgaria.

On 18th January 1919 the Allies met at the Paris Peace Conference to work out a peace settlement which was signed by Germany. It became known as **The Treaty of Versailles**.

Key Dates

1914

28 June	Archduke Franz Ferdinand assassinated
28 July	Austria-Hungary declares war on Serbia
1 Aug	Germany declares war on Russia
3 Aug	Germany declares war on France and invades Belgium
4 Aug	Britain declares war on Germany
5 Aug	Austria-Hungary declares war on Russia
6 Aug	Serbia declares war on Germany
10 Aug	France declares war on Austria-Hungary
12 Aug	Britain declares war on Austria-Hungary
6 Sept	First Battle of Marne begins
27 Sept	Russians invade Hungary
10 Oct	First Battle of Ypres begins
3 Nov	Russia declares war on Turkey
5 Nov	Britain and France declare war on Turkey

1915

22 Apr	Germans first use poison gas at Ypres
25 Apr	Allied forces land at Gallipoli
7 May	U-boat sinks British Lusitania
23 May	Italy declares war on Turkey
15 Oct	Britain declares war on Bulgaria

1916

21 Feb	Battle of Verdun begins
9 Mar	Germany declares war on Portugal
31 May	Battle of Jutland
1 July	Allies launch Somme offensive; 60,000 British casualties on first day
4 Aug	Italy declares war on Germany

1917

March	Revolution begins in Russia
6 Apr	USA declares war on Germany
31 July	Passchendaele offensive begun by British
14 Aug	China declares war on Germany and Austria-Hungary
5 Dec	Russia and Germany sign armistice
7 Dec	USA declares war on Austria-Hungary

1918

3 Mar	Treaty of Brest-Litovsk
22 July	Allies cross Marne beginning decisive counter-offensive
9 Nov	Kaiser Wilhelm II abdicates
11 Nov	Germany and Allies sign armistice

First World War Slang

Tommy, Tommies – or 'Poor Bloody Tommy Atkins'
Ordinary British Soldiers

'Jerry', 'Old Fritz', 'The Boche', 'The Hun'
The Germans or German Soldiers

'Blighty' or 'Dear Old Blighty'
Britain

'A Blighty One'
A wound that would get you sent home to Britain
('Blighty' comes from an old Indian word meaning 'being
away from where you belong', picked up by British
troops in the days of the British Raj in India)

'No Mans Land'
**The strip of land between two armies and not under
the control of either one**

Demob. or demobilisation
**Being discharged from the army at the end of
one's service**

*W.W.I, 'The Great War' 1st World War
'The War to end all Wars'*
The 1914–1918 War

'Over the top'
**To climb up and over the side of a trench
and charge towards the enemy**

James 'Smiler' Lovegrove
(Age 95)

James 'Smiler' Lovegrove (1993)

The author with 'Smiler' during one of many interviews

'Smiler' in 1917

As I read through the Readers' Letters section of a daily newspaper I noticed one titled 'How you do not always feel pain', written by an old soldier of the First World War. He said he had been shot while fighting in the trenches but did not realise it until sometime later. At once I started the job of locating the writer of that letter and this led eventually to my meeting with a most charming gentleman, Mr. James 'Smiler' Lovegrove, ninety-five years old, and living in a rest home situated in a refined suburb of Eastbourne.

As we sat in his quiet room looking across the bay to Beachy Head I could not help but be impressed by this slightly built, frail man, immaculately dressed, who could hold one's attention for ages with the most fascinating conversation. As we became friends, during the space of several visits, I realised what a trusting man he is, giving me items of great personal value, to take away with me to study in depth: photograph albums, letters, all from the Edwardian and World War I era.

There was enough for a book on 'Smiler' alone. As we sat talking it became obvious how he got his nickname. He did, of course, smile a lot, but more than this his whole personality was relaxed and engaging. I could also see how such a manner could enable him to cope with, and indeed, get through such an horrendous experience as World War I. Maybe behind such easygoing pleasantness lay a great personal strength, because, incredibly, he joined as a private and came out over four years later as an officer. I listened with great interest as to how this was achieved and switched on my tape recorder...

Question: "Tell me about your early years 'Smiler'."

Answer: "Well I grew up in South London. We were a big middle-class family. Father was a master tailor, had a shop in Mayfair. He was a clever man, wrote books on Eastern religions and was very talented at his craft. He made a lot of money but never knew how to manage it, so he died penniless. I recall when I was a child, must have been around 1907, he bought a huge motorcar, a French 'Vosin', I think it was. You could drive all day and never see another car. We did feel grand, until he ran into the gates of Hyde Park!"

Q: "How old were you when war started?"

A: "Sixteen. My parents used to worry about me. I was not very strong and often ill during my childhood, so my father got me into an office job with a firm of architects in the Kingsway in London. Well, on my way to work one morning a group of women surrounded me. They started shouting and yelling at me, calling me all sorts of names for not being a soldier! D'you know what they did? They stuck a white feather in my coat, meaning I was a coward. Oh, I did feel dreadful, so ashamed.

So that night, to cheer myself up, I went to the music hall. The star of the show was Vesta Tilly, a great star of the time. She'd come on stage dressed as a soldier, singing patriotic songs, then she would invite men up onto the stage to join up and 'take the king's shilling'. Of course, there were a couple of recruiting sergeants standing ready in the wings. Now she was married to a conservative M.P., Lord de Frece, and she got so many men into the army this way there was even a 'Vesta Tilly Brigade' fighting in France. Yet she had the nerve to refuse to go over and entertain the troops like many other artists did saying she couldn't spare the time. But after the war she found the time to retire to Monte Carlo!"

Q: "Did you volunteer, Smiler?"

A: "Yes, silly young fool that I was. Then along with hundreds of others, I was taken to the recruiting office. The sergeant there couldn't stop laughing at me, saying things like 'Looking for your father, sonny?', and 'Come back next year when the war's over!' Well, I must have looked so crestfallen that he said, 'Let's check your measurements again'. You see, I was five foot six inches and only about eight and half stone. This time he made me out to be about six feet tall and twelve stone, at least, that is what he wrote down. All lies of course – but I was in!"

Q: "Where were you sent to first?"

A: "Woolwich Common, six hundred of us, sleeping under tents, in the middle of winter. I'll never forget my first night in the army. Mother had always told me to wear pyjamas or I'd get lumbago! Well, I was putting them on when the tent flap opened and a voice said 'Cor bloody blimey! Come and 'ave a look at this bloke, he's getting dressed to go to bed!' Well, they all had a good laugh at me. I don't think most of them had seen pyjamas before. They all seemed to sleep naked. And the foul language! I'd never heard such swearing before in my life. I just cringed and went to sleep.

Next morning, on my first parade the Corporal told me to go over to the barracks and dry scrub the floor. Well, I'd been told to laugh at his jokes, so I did. Next thing I knew I was on the floor! He'd given me a real 'fourpenny one'. So I went off and found myself a quiet corner and cried my eyes out. Well, he knew he'd done wrong by hitting me so he came looking for me and said 'Lovegrove, I don't like being laughed at.' I said I'd never heard of a dry scrubber and I thought he was joking.

He was O.K after that, even gave me a pass so I could go home for the evening, so I hopped on the tram to show off my new uniform to the folks. It wasn't a very good fit. It almost drowned me. When He saw it father said 'Good God Almighty, you never came through the streets looking like that did you? Take it off at once and I'll alter it for you.' And he did, bless him ... Mind you, next day on parade I was fined for defacing government property. One of the officers noticed it had been altered."

Q: "Being a quiet lad, how did you get on, mixing with crowds of men?"

A: "Oh, fine. You meet all sorts. Many were glad to be in because they'd been unemployed and hungry, no dole money then, you see. One of my pals had been in the navy and was blown up at the Battle of Jutland. As a result of that he was half deaf. He was Buster Brown, cruiser weight boxing champion. Now, unable to read or write, deaf and no pension from the navy, he was sleeping rough with nowhere to go. As he used to say 'I hate the army, but at least they feed me.' And there were many like him."

Q: "What sort of training did they give you for war?"

A: "Well, first I was in the Royal Field Artillery, but then got transferred to a Cavalry Regiment. The army were still thinking in terms of horse warfare, cavalry charges with lances and swords! The ones running the war were so backward and out of date, it was ridiculous – no, worse than that, it was murderous."

Q: "Could you ride a horse? Is that why you were put in the Cavalry?"

A: "No, never been on a horse in my life. The first day we were told to mount up, take hold of the reins, put our feet in the stirrups, then the officer said 'Dig your heels in', and off you'd go. We went all right. Those horses threw us all over the place. We all ended up on the ground. Then we were charged with dismounting without orders! These horses were sent over in large numbers from the Argentine. At least a third of each consignment had to be put down. They arrived in a dreadful state. Somebody somewhere was making a fortune out of it. We heard reports from France of cavalry charges against German machine-guns. The slaughter was unbelievable. The mud was so bad you could sink up to your knees in it. Thick soaking wet clay, so imagine a horse and rider trying to gallop! Ten yards and they'd come to a stop and be shot to bits. There were so many dead men and horses. They used them to fill the shell craters so lorries could be driven across."

(At this point 'Smiler' became upset and began to cry as he recalled these horrendous memories, so we took a break and came back to it a few days later).

Q: "So, Smiler, did you go from Woolwich straight to France?"

A: "No, Ireland, to put down the rebellion. We were lucky to reach Cork, because German submarines chased our ship all the way over. One escorting gunboat got sunk. Anyway, by the time we got there the rebellion was over! But the Irish hated us, and were so aggressive towards us. We were not allowed outside the camp. It was worse than being at war. Every minute was spent in training and parades. The discipline was very strict. Week after week was spent in firing the '303 rifle. I'd never fired a gun until then, but after months of training I passed out a crack shot, what they called a 'Marksman'. I was starting to find my feet, so to speak. I was such a silly little boy when I first joined, I just didn't know anything, and I was so skinny and weak. But I got on with everyone because I trusted everyone. I still do: or try to."

Q: "How long were you in Ireland?"

A: "About a year, I think. Then the colonel sent for me and said 'I'm thinking of making you a corporal, Lovegrove, as you have been recommended for promotion'. Then he asked 'Do you smoke, drink, swear or go out with women?' I replied 'No Sir, I don't'. 'Well', he said 'you'd be no good as a corporal. I'll send you on an officers course instead'. Well everyone laughed, but the next thing I knew, I was on the train to Belfast to train as an officer."

Q: "To recap Smiler, what regiment were you now in?"

A: "While in Ireland we were moved from cavalry to infantry, but now I was on my way to France as a lieutenant in the 1st Battalion Royal North Lancashire Regiment."

Q: "Whereabouts in France were you sent?"

A: "We were moving up to take part in the battle for the Drocourt Queant switch-line on the Somme. I am the last known survivor of that battle."

Q: "What were conditions like when you got there?"

A: "The public have never, even to this day, been told how bad it was for the men. No words could adequately describe the horror of it all.

I am ashamed to say the officers were fed reasonably, but the men were starving. Living conditions were so filthy that I got enteric fever, was put into a field-hospital and almost died. There was so much illness of every sort amongst us. It was truly hell on earth. Lice, rats, trench foot – that's gangrenous condition that the men got through standing in wet mud that we lived in. And trench mouth, where the gums rot and you lose your teeth. And of course dead bodies everywhere. Also the mental fear of the dreaded sniper who'd take your head off in a flash if you so much as looked over the top of the trench.

The slaughter was beyond belief. The French army alone had lost three hundred thousand men and that was only up to the end of 1915. But that total was more than doubled the next year at the battle of Verdun, and just as many Germans died in that battle too. And further north where we were headed on the Somme, the Germans and us lost around half a million men."

Q: "God, these are awful figures just to write down, figures like these are beyond understanding."

A: "I know, I know, look at it this way, on July 1st 1916, that was the first day of the battle of the Somme, the British Army suffered twenty thousand dead and twice that number badly wounded..."

Q: "And that's just one day?"

A: "Yes. The military commanders had no respect for human life. General Douglas Haig, later he was made a Field Marshal, cared nothing about casualties. Of course, he was carrying out government policy, because after the war, he was knighted and given a lump sum and a massive life-pension. I blame the public schools who bred these ego maniacs. They should never have been in charge of men. Never...

The whole system seem to be geared to punish the ordinary soldier. For example, it was undesirable, of course, but there were a lot of brothels in the French towns so V.D. was at epidemic proportions. In fact it was estimated by the Royal Army Medical Corps that during the 14–18 war a quarter of the armies in Europe were incapacitated by gonorrhoea and syphilis. Now, if a man reported sick with any V.D. type illness his pay, and even worse, his allowance home to his wife, was stopped. You can imagine the misery that caused. Plus, any leave that he may have had due was also stopped. My sergeant caught a dose, just when he was about to go on leave. Well, I got a letter from his wife asking why he'd not come home. I wrote back saying he was one of my most important men and I couldn't spare him for a few weeks. Mind you, I had no answer as to why his pay had stopped."

Q: "Tell me how you got shot".

A: "Well, we were ordered to attack a German trench so we fell in behind a tank for cover, but the tank got a direct hit by a shell. It spun round on its tracks and burst into flames. The crew were roasted alive. They couldn't get out. Somehow we made it to the German trench, their machine-gunners were all lying dead next to their guns. Our big gun barrage before our advance had killed them. I noticed they were fixed to their guns by a length of chain so they could not run away. I suppose their high command was as bad as ours. Our lads had not eaten in days so they started eating the German rations because they were starving.

Then my commanding officer was killed by a sniper, so I took over. A shout went up 'The huns are counter attacking'. I could see crowds of them swarming across the open ground towards us with fixed bayonets. I grabbed a Mills grenade and threw it but in my panic I fumbled it and it landed on the ledge of the trench. By now they were in the far end of the trench and running towards us. We fled into the next bay. As 'jerry' passed where my grenade was it went off, killing many of them. They were a brave lot. They came on, throwing stick-bombs as they ran. One of my best men tried to pick one up as it landed to throw it back, but it blew his hand off and both his eyes out. When I saw that, I just couldn't stop being sick – awful, just awful. We were now trapped in the far end of the trench. Some of the lads panicked and tried to climb out. All those who did fell back dead, shot between the eyes by German snipers. We could only keep our heads down and pray.

After an hour or so, the Germans pulled out. They'd seen a sergeant with a large squad of tommies in the distance looking for us.

I had a batman chap whose surname was Rose. He got plenty of leg pulling about that. He was old to be in the trenches, must have been turned forty, as many of the men were. He was like an older brother to me. He saved my life a couple of times.

Anyway, during this lull I decided to take the men back to one of our empty trenches, but we'd lost all sense of direction, what with noise and gun-smoke all around us, and we came under fire. I got knocked clear off my feet. When I tried to stand I just kept falling over. Rose said 'Can't see any blood or damage, sir, let's crawl the rest of the way.' We did and fell into the trench. About six of us made it back. As we sat there exhausted, Rose put his fingers to his lips and said 'Quiet, there are German voices coming from down that dugout, if they hear us we're dead'. It was a German trench, you see, that we had mistakenly got into."

Q: "How did you get out of that?"

A: "Well, insane as it sounds, I threw my last Mills bomb down the steps. I'll never forget the sound of it bouncing all the way down. Then the explosion and the chilling sound of screams. How many were killed I'll never know. Three came charging up at us with fixed bayonets. One of our boys got stabbed through the neck, died at once. The hand to hand fighting lasted a few minutes, we killed all three. I wasn't much help. I could only stand on one leg. Anyway, thirty one more came up and surrendered. They'd had enough. So had we, come to that.

Rose got me on a stretcher and made the Germans carry me back to base hospital. I kept my revolver pointed at their officer in case they led us into a trap. Once at the base the Germans were marched off to a prison camp. It was only then I realised my gun was empty. Rose thought that was hilarious. He should have stayed with me but wanted to get back to our platoon and got killed on the way back. I recommended him for a medal but it was refused.

It turned out I'd been shot through the ankle and all the bones had been smashed. Once I was told that, the pain started like hell. I was sent to the American hospital in Boulogne for an operation. After some weeks it was back to 'Blighty' for me to convalesce."

Q: "Did you get a war pension for your wounds?"

A: "No, nothing. I was still in hospital in London on November 11th, 1918 when the armistice was signed and it was all over and we had peace, but only for twenty-one years. Then it all started again, and I was back in uniform for ten years, 1939–49."

Q: "So by now, Smiler, you must have had enough of war?"

A: "I have indeed, Terry, because you know at heart my generation were a peaceful lot who placed great store in graceful living, good manners and kindness, but 14–18 wiped that off the face of the earth forever."

After the Second World War Smiler settled down with his wife and two young sons to become a respected business man.

Note: Sadly, as this book was on its way to the printers I received news from one of his sons that my friend Smiler had passed away peacefully in his sleep aged 96. That charming man with the friendly smile will be sadly missed.

James 'Smiler' Lovegrove (left) with two brothers in 1914.
One looks too young even to lie about his age.

One of the earliest recruiting posters from 1914 displayed
mainly in the North and in Scotland.

The famous 'Kitchener' poster on show in every main street
on hoardings, in newspapers, trams, etc.

Trench life.

W. Sherrard-Smith M.C.
(Age 97)

Lt. Col. Sherrard-Smith

A relative told me about a man who lived in the same block of flats as he. This man in his nineties could be seen jogging around the gardens every morning. He was apparently an ex-Army man, who had fought in both World Wars. I at once wrote to him to arrange a meeting. Back came a typed formal letter agreeing to see me in a week or so.

My contact turned out to be Lt.Col. W. Sherrard-Smith M.C. living in a quiet and secluded modern flat with his third wife. His manner was polite but also formal and correct. At ninety-seven years old he was in amazingly good health, apart from poor sight in one of his eyes. Tea was already laid on and ready to serve. After the tea had brewed for exactly four minutes a small alarm bell set on the tray began to ring. "Tea must stand for just four minutes", explained the Colonel. "No more, no less. I know, having lived in India d'you see." I thought it best to agree. He then explained that in my letter to him requesting a meeting I had made a spelling mistake. My next mistake was to put my small tape recorder on the table. I use it at interviews so that I can recall what people have said. The Colonel did not like the idea. My wife then asked if she could take some photos. He was not keen but relented, possibly because of her blue eyes, as he admitted himself – "I still have an eye for the ladies, d'you see!" He personified the old Indian 'Raj', strict, autocratic, ruthless and intelligent, yet charmingly cultured and correct.

Since leaving the Army some forty-three years ago he has turned with zest to other endeavours, having written several books on health, covering diet, exercise, etc. I told him what a good advert he was for his own books. He replied – "Health is everything. This world today won't carry any wounded. It was hard enough in my day but now if you fall behind you'd better get a comrade to shoot you." While I pondered that remark, he went on to say "I wouldn't like to be a youngster today. They have material things, of course, but not much else." His views on the past seemed to be very clear cut. He bore no ill will to his old enemies. In fact, he respected as soldiers the Germans and Italians. He also had respect for the Japanese forces but tempered with fear, as a fanatical and fearsome fighting force who came within an inch of taking over the whole of Asia.

He was obviously a man who was mentally very strong and who regretted nothing. He had always done his duty to the best of his ability. I could not help but feel that had I been, in the 1920's, a rifleman pinned down by gunfire, trapped behind a rock in the scorching heat, waiting for Indian tribesmen to move in for the kill. Or in the 1940's, a Tommie lying wounded on the deck of a freighter while the Japanese air force tried to blow us out of the water, I would have been pleased to have had the Colonel in charge. I'd know instinctively that this hundred per cent professional would somehow get us out, and as he did so, I'd feel ashamed of all those names that I had called him under my breath whilst on parade or on a route march. I nervously switched on my tape recorder and began the interview.

Question: "Where did you spend your childhood, Colonel?"

Answer: "India, born and grew up there. My father was from London and in the British Civil Service. I was studying agriculture but got into the Army as soon as I could. Joined up in 1916. Went into the 1st 55th Colt Rifles, better known as the 'Piffers'. That's their nickname. I stayed with them right through to the end. We were fighting in German East Africa, transferred there from our H.Q base on the N.W. Frontier of

India. You see, in those days the British Empire was enormous, and the Germans had a massive Empire as well. That's really what the War was about. They thought we were over extended and had weak leadership at home so decided we were ripe for a takeover. You see, with our Empire and their own they would have had effective control of the whole world at that time. We were up against crack German divisions but we could call on African and Indian reserves, as many as we needed. But they were short of manpower because they had always treated the Africans so badly that whole platoons of men would disappear or run away into the bush and the jungle. But for all that the Germans were a crack fighting force. It was a hellish and bloody conflict."

Q: "And you got your first wound in Africa?"

A: "Yes, got shot in the head." (He pointed to a deep scar on his forehead). "The bullet lodged in the bone and it knocked me out of the War for almost two years. I didn't expect to survive that one, but here I am today, and that bullet hit me in 1918. Then in the 1920's I was fighting up on the N.W. Frontier in India. I always regarded that as the best fighting of all. You were up against a very clever enemy. The tribesmen on that frontier were brave and fanatical, they got most of their armaments from Russia. But later we found 'Made in Birmingham' stamped on their guns. The same as ours."

Q: "And you were awarded the Military Cross at that time?"

A: "Yes. Couple of my men were wounded and pinned down in open country. We were trying to get to the top of a hill strewn with large boulders. The tribesmen were firing down on us, very difficult, d'you see? Anyway, I told my men to give me covering fire and dashed out, grabbed one of the wounded

– he died later poor chap – then I went out for the other one and got hit but managed to get us both back to cover. But the bullets had gone right through my body, hitting me in the side and coming out via my hip, and d'you know, only eight years ago I had to go into hospital to have part of a bullet taken out of my back. The surgeon told me it had been travelling around my body all those years.

But that was the best type of fighting because you're fighting on your feet, d'you see? In those days, in the First World War and in the 20's and 30's mules carried your baggage, ammo, small arms, machine guns, etc. In the Second World War trucks and other vehicles, like half tracks, did all that. In World War I you would be shot by a rifle bullet or even a hand gun. But in World War II you'd be blown to bits by a shell fired from many miles away."

Q: "And you fought in World War II?"

A: "Oh my word yes. I fought the Japs when they took Malaya. The Japanese Imperial Army were an incredible fighting force that showed no mercy to anyone who stood in its way. They pushed us right down to Singapore. I was at a meeting of officers one day and the Colonel said – Gentlemen, this is going to be the longest siege in the history of the British Army. I replied – 'Sir, with respect that's rubbish, they will be here within two days.' And they were. I got badly wounded, was put on a boat to Java. From there I was transferred to a Red Cross ship. The day after we sailed from Java the Japs arrived. I count myself very lucky not to have been a prisoner of the Japs. And it was lucky for the West and the Allies that the Americans got hold of the atomic bomb before they did. Japan, d'you see, wanted all the old British interests in the Pacific area like Australia and New Zealand, and, of course, all of Asia."

Q: "You've had an adventurous life, Colonel."

A: "Oh my word yes. The Army gave me a wonderful life. Fought all over the world, except Europe. My son, he joined up in the Second World War and retired just a few years ago with the rank of Colonel. I was inspecting a troop train once in India when this young teenager came up to me and shook hands. Well, I was surprised and said 'How do you do? But who are you?' And this lad said – don't you know me father? Good Lord, d'you know, it was my son from England, I'd not seen him for about 7 or 8 years! I never got home to England on leave much between the Wars."

Q: "When did you leave the Army?"

A: "1949, aged 55. I left India the day they were granted independence. I was glad to leave. It wasn't the India I knew anymore, and of course the Empire had shrunk so much, and today it's gone completely. I knew and met all the leaders of India except this present chap Rajiv Gandhi who's recently been assassinated."

Q: "Did you meet Mahatma Gandhi?"

A: "Oh yes, a wonderful man, very clever, he understood everything. He liked us British. Wanted to be friends with us. But also wanted us out of his country. Can't blame him for that, can you! I often wonder what India's like now. All those lovely churches and cathedrals that were there at that time. I wonder if they were kept up and maintained when we left. I doubt it."

Q: "You've led an exciting but dangerous life, Colonel, and having been wounded seven times, you have known a lot of pain. Are you happy at this time of your life?"

A: "Oh yes. I make myself, d'you see. I do a little woodwork, (he showed me a small table and other items he had made). I do miss my reading. I used to read a great deal, but I am almost blind in my right eye. And I have Tinnitus, a constant ringing in my head, as a result of my head wound. But, I believe in mind over matter. I don't dwell on 'ifs' or maybe's', always stick to facts, try and put problems to the back of your mind. No-one can really help you in this life. You have to master yourself. Never let anyone master you. You must conquer yourself. D'you see? It's the only way to peace of mind."

He then took pride in showing me his Military Cross and many other campaign medals, and other items of great military interest. After an hour or so spent talking of many things he walked with me to the car park to see us of.

"I gave up driving a couple of years ago", he said. "No manners on the road nowadays."

As I thanked him for his time and help, I just stopped myself from calling him by his first name. It would not have been right somehow.

"Goodbye, Colonel, and thank you so much."

"That's quite all right, old chap, I've enjoyed talking to you. One thing, though,"

"Yes Sir?"

"Do brush up on your spelling. All wrong to have a writer who can't spell, d'you see."

As we drove away my wife remarked "You'll not see his like again."

"How true", I replied ..."How very true."

William Brooks
(Age 94)

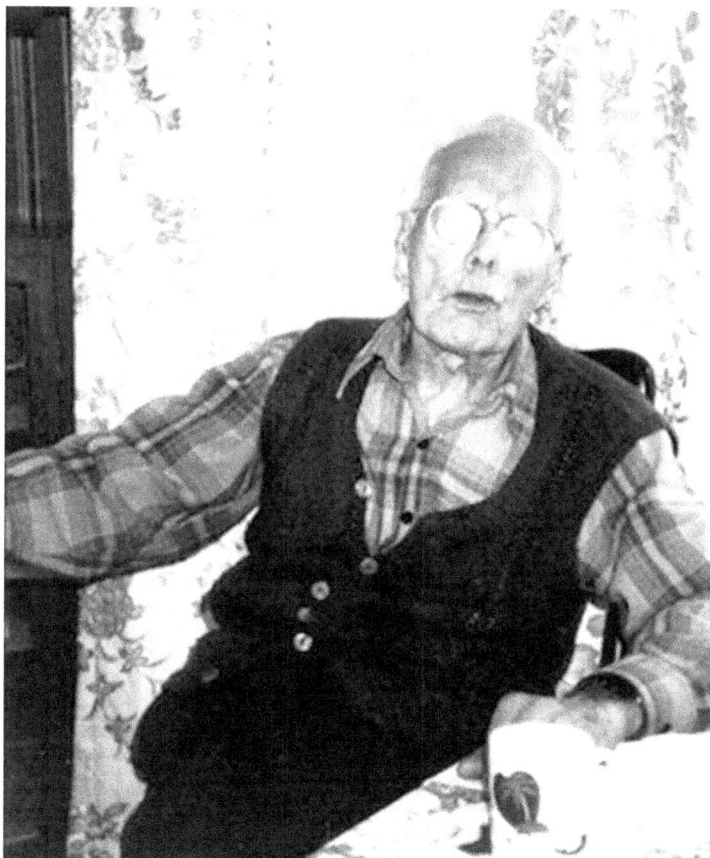

Bill Brooks, aged 94

A pal of mine in the British Legion telephoned me about William (Bill) Brooks. "He's been a member of our branch for years," he said, "I've told him you'd like to call for a chat about the First World War. He's a great old chap, ninety-four-years-old, served all though the fourteen-eighteen lot. Anyway, he's expecting you, so call round anytime."

He then gave me directions on how to get to Bill's place. I found the house tucked away down a quiet country lane on the outskirts of a small market town. It was a warm summer's day as my wife Patricia and I approached the open street door.

"Anyone home?" I called out rather self-consciously.

"I'm in here, cutting wood," replied a strong voice, coming from a nearby garden shed. As I entered I could barely see because compared to the bright sunlight outside, the interior of the shed was in almost total darkness. I could just make out the figure of a tall well-built man. He exchanged friendly greetings and introductions, yet he ignored my outstretched hand. I then realised that he was almost blind.

"I've just been chopping up some firewood ready for the winter," he said. I noticed the razor-sharp axe.

"Christ, man, you'll cut your fingers off!"

"No need to worry," he said, "my sense of touch is probably better than your eyesight."

We headed into the house, Bill confidently leading the way. "I've lived here over forty years, so I know every inch of the place."

"Do you live here alone?"

"Yes," he replied, "I love the place. No 'old peoples' home for me. I am here 'till I drop. I value my independence above all else. I've been expecting you and I've got out a few things to show you, medals and photos, all from World War I."

So, to the sound of birds singing in his lovely garden, we sat down to a nicely laid out tea and began the interview.

Question: "Tell me, Bill, where were you born, and where did you grow up?"

Answer: "Born in London, grew up in Woolwich. My dad was a seaman in the Merchant Navy. I was very close to my dad, we were the best of pals. At fifteen I went to work at the Woolwich Arsenal. It was a huge place in those days, it employed thousands. I was serving an apprenticeship to become an iron and steel moulder. But once war broke out the situation at home became awful, because people didn't like to see men or lads of army age walking about in civilian clothing, or not in a uniform of some sort, especially in a military town like Woolwich. Women were the worst. They would come up to you in the street and give you a white feather, or stick it in the lapel of your coat."

Q: "What did they mean by doing that?"

A: "Well, a white feather is the sign of cowardice, so they meant you were a coward and that you should be in the army doing your bit for king and country. It got so bad it wasn't safe to go out. So in 1915 at the age of seventeen I volunteered under the 'Lord Darby' scheme. Now that was a thing where once you applied to join you were not called up at once, but were given a blue armband with a red crown to wear. This told people that you were waiting to be called up, and that kept you safe, or fairly safe, because if you were seen to be wearing it for too long the abuse in the street would soon start again."

Q: "People must have been very anti-German then?"

A: "Oh Lord, yes. War fever was sweeping the country. Mind you, the press were responsible for that, there was no TV or radio of course, so the newspapers got people ready for war. It was like an hysteria, a madness. In a way the government controlled the people – via Fleet Street."

Q: "Did you have to wait long, Bill, before being called up?"

A: "No, just a few weeks, then I was put in the Royal Army Service Corps and, would you believe, the horse transport section – and I never knew one end of a horse from the other! Once they realised their mistake I was moved to the R.E's (Royal Engineers). My wage was seventeen shillings per week, and there were women at the Arsenal earning four pounds per week working on munitions. Mind you, they had to work an eighty-hour seven-day week."

Q: "When did you go abroad?"

A: "Sent to France in January, 1917, to work on the broad-gauge railway. That was the railway system that took all manner of supplies, mainly ammunitions and guns, also food up to the front line, and sadly the same trains would bring back the dead. Hundreds and hundreds of them. Now to give you an idea how badly paid the British tommies were, I got six pence a day overseas allowance. We worked alongside South African soldiers and a Royal South African sergeant got fifteen shillings a day! It was very hard non-stop work maintaining that railway system, but it was essential to the war. I was mainly 'casting' – making everything from five-foot high wheels for steam trains to engine-blocks for trucks. The South Africans were mining experts and they built a whole network of tunnels, about six foot high and ten foot wide. These had a narrow-gauge railway system inside them, plus most of our workshops and living quarters. The Germans, of course, knew this and we suffered frequent bombing raids, but the S.A.'s designed the tunnel system in such a clever way that when a bomb hit one tunnel you could, if you'd not been injured, run into the next one. And all the tunnels were linked at the back by a long and very deep one that could withstand a direct hit."

Q: "What was discipline like?"

A: "Very strict, but we were lucky. We had a 'one in a million' Colonel, Colonel Cole, a great chap who cared about his men."

Q: "Why, Bill, what did he do?"

A: "Well, one thing, in our work in the foundry we got filthy. After a long day's work the dirt was ground into you. This Colonel was very ahead of his time and he had hot showers installed for the men, very primitive, not like today's ones of course, but by God we were grateful for them."

Q: "Whereabouts was this, Bill?"

A: "A place called Rouen, in France. We never suffered a direct attack by German troops, it was all air attack, and we couldn't fight back much because we were so desperately short of ammo. It all had to go up to the front-line, you see. We had one anti-aircraft gun mounted on a train that we kept in the siding. It could be fired while on the move along the tracks but we'd only have three or four shells. Once we'd used them we had to dash for cover into the tunnels until old Fritz' cleared off! Of course, he had a field day, blowing up the tracks and the rolling stock. If we'd been attacked by foot soldiers it would have been the end of us because all we had were Lee Enfield '303 rifles with short bayonets, but no ammo, so we couldn't fire a shot."

Q: "What about leave, did you ever get any?"

A: "Not much. Once in a while we were allowed into Rouen to have a drink, and in four years I got one leave home for two weeks. That was marvellous, to see my family again, and especially dear old dad. Now, that's a strange thing. Dad gave up being a sailor in 1913 but when war started a year later in 1914 he was called up to serve in the Military Marines. He was born in 1863 so he must have been fifty-one years old when war started. I remember the police coming to the house and telling him to report to Portsmouth. My mother was heartbroken. She had looked forward so much to him coming home for good. You see, they mounted heavy guns on the decks of all the passenger liners and a platoon of marines on board. Dad was on the Cape Town run, very dangerous because of German U-boats, but he got through the war safely, bless him."

Q: "Were your family still in Woolwich at this time?"

A: "Dad had bought a house in nearby Eltham. He loved that house. He was always painting it. He died in 1939 and during World War II in 1942 it got blown to bits by a German bomb. I'm glad he never lived to see that.

But getting back to that leave, that's where I met my future wife, Marjorie, in Greenwich Park. I was with a pal and she had a friend with her. They were listening to the band and we all got chatting. Then we went out together everyday for the rest of my leave. She was very sad at the time, though."

Q: "Why was that?"

A: "Well, she was a nurse and was treating men who had been gassed in the trenches with mustard gas. That burns the inside of the lungs and those poor men were suffering the dreadful effects. Majorie told me they were in agony and would scream out all night long, but there was next to nothing anyone could do for them. One night, we watched a Zeppelin raid on the Woolwich Arsenal. The German Zeppelin was sort of hovering over the building dropping bombs and they scored a couple of direct hits, causing massive explosions. We felt the blast two to three miles away. A few small bi-planes of ours went up to attack it but the Zep. had heavy machine-guns mounted in the cabin slung beneath it and, being almost stationary, could take careful aim on a 'plane. So our brave airmen stood no chance. But one little 'plane went up, one of those double wing ones with all the struts holding the wings together, you know the sort. Well, this pilot flew above the Zep. And dropped bombs down onto it. One hit it square on – flames started to light up the night sky. She was on fire all right. Everyone in the street started to cheer. My dad was watching through a small telescope he had and said he could see the men on the Zep. inside the cabin rushing about throwing ropes over the side and other things, trying to lighten the ship. Anyway, its main engines started up with a roar and she slowly began to move away with smoke pouring out of her – and a strange thing – the crew pulled in the German flag so that it was flying at half-mast."

Q: "Why, what did that mean?"

A: "Well, dad said they knew they were done for, but were going to try and make it home. As it pulled away it looked like a huge wounded animal going home to die."

Q: "Did they make it back to Germany?"

A: "No, they crashed in flames over Essex before they made the Channel. I know they were our enemies but I couldn't help feeling sorry for them. That was the last of the Zep. Raids. They proved too vulnerable. The pilot of our small 'plane was a Lt.Robinson and he got the V.C., that's the Victoria Cross for that, but the poor man was shot down and killed over France a year later by an ace German fighter-pilot.

On my return to France the war was starting to go in our favour, mainly because the Americans had come in on our side. Mind you, the Yanks and the Aussies were disgusted at the way our officers treated us. There were cases where British officers tried to put Yanks or Aussie soldiers in front of a firing-squad, but couldn't get away with it. If they had, I reckon those countries would have pulled out of the war and left us to it. There was a big riot about September 1917 by the Australians at a place called Etaples. They called it 'collective indiscipline', what it was was mutiny. It went on for days. I think a couple of military police got killed. Field Marshal Haig would have shot the leaders but dared not of course because they were Aussies. Haig's nickname was 'the butcher'. He'd think nothing of sending thousands of men to certain death.

By now we had hundreds of Prisoners of War working at our depot, mainly Germans. The Saxons were O.K, but the Prussians were very arrogant, mind you, they were all glad to be our prisoners. They were terrified of the French and the Australians who treated them very badly. And as for the Russians! Do you know, many Germans killed themselves rather than be taken prisoner by the Russians. We had German P.O.W's sent to us from the Russian front and they were so ill and weak they could not lift a spade. Suffering from starvation and ill-treatment, you see."

Q: "Can you recall any other sort of personal memories, Bill?"

A: "Well, I don't know. It's all so long, long ago. It is the little things that come back to you, things that did not seem terribly important at the time. We had one German prisoner, a big chap called Otto, and one day, after years, these poor devils got some mail from home via the Red Cross. He opened his letter. It had been written about eighteen months before by his wife and she had sent her photo. Well, he got so excited. 'Look, look, Tommie', he shouted. He gave me the letter to read, but of course, I couldn't read German, so he read it to me. It was just some news from home. Then Otto sat down and cried for hours. No one said anything. I think we all understood how he felt, British or German."

Q: "How did you manage after your discharge, with poor eyesight?"

A: "I couldn't return to my old trade, but I managed to get a job with Harrods Department Store in London, in their furniture removals department, and stayed with them for nearly thirty years. And do you know, one of our best customers was Gen. Haig (the butcher). He was always buying expensive furniture, but all the men working as removers who had served in the war refused to touch anything to do with him. They had to get another firm to deliver it and they told me that on the big gates outside his mansion he had statues of doves, the bird of peace. Him, of all people! It would be funny if it wasn't so tragic."

Q: "What's your main impression, or feeling, regarding the war, Bill, when you look back on it all?"

A: "The utter waste and disregard for human life and human suffering by the so-called educated classes who ran the country. What a wicked waste of life. I'd hate to be in their shoes when they face their Maker..."

As I concluded the interview Bill told us that a great grandchild was due to visit him from the U.S.A. He was looking forward to the visit and wanted to get the place tidied up. I noticed the great care with which he replaced the photos into the album, especially those of his father and his wife who had died only two years ago.

"You must miss them very much, Bill," I said.

"Yes, that's true, but I speak to them every day. I know they're with me in spirit. In fact, I can see them more clearly in my mind's eye than I can see you with my real eyes."

We laughed as we shook hands to say goodbye, but that laughter rang with truth.

A few days after the interview I got a 'phone call from Bill. "I've been thinking about your book," he said. "Don't mind my asking, but would it be possible to include a picture of my dad? It would mean so much to me if you could. He was the best of fathers and I've always been proud of him."

"I'll make sure of it, Bill", I replied. "After all, he served throughout the war even though he was in his fifties, so he deserves a mention, it's the least we can do".

Bill Brooks (1916)

Bill Brook's father
circa 1915

> *"The 1914–18 war was the first war in history that involved the whole world. It was, in fact The First 'World' War – The Great War – the war to end all wars."*
> **Sir John French , British Field Marshall in 14–18 War.**

> *"Never again will armies of such vast size and strength face each other on the field of battle."*
> **Sir WinstonChurchill, First Lord of the Admiralty in World War I, Prime Minister and War Leader in World War II.**

> *"The military leaders on both sides showed a total and wicked disregard for human life and suffering, and are completely without compassion. These war-mongering generals who sent our young men to their deaths will live to a safe old age, you can be sure of that."*
> **A statement made by my grandfather. I never knew him. He died the year I was born. He died as a result of being 'called up' when in his mid-thirties with five young children at home and spending two years as a Prisoner of War in Germany. (The Author).**

German war leader, General Ludendorff,
died 1937 aged 72.

Count Von Hindenburg, German Field Marshal, died
1934, aged 87.

Earl Douglas Haig, Commander-in-Chief of the British
Forces in France, died 1928 aged 67.

Sir John French, British Field Marshal,
died 1925 aged 73.

Charles Young
(Age 93)

Charles Young on a visit to the war graves in France

Charles Young (right) at an Armistice Day service

I travelled across London to meet Mr. Charles Young and met a cheerful man who could pass for seventy instead of his ninety-three years. The most striking part of his personality is his cheerfulness and his conversation carries warmth and friendliness. This disposition must, of course, hide an extremely tough nature because he went through the entire fourteen-eighteen war and the hell of the battles like Ypres, Passchendaele and the Somme. He saw many comrades get killed and got badly wounded himself on two separate occasions.

Yet, when recalling these monstrous events he tended to focus on the small things that brought a smile to his face, things that gave the men a much needed laugh at the time. This could lead the casual observer to believe we were discussing a pleasant subject, or an unimportant topic, instead of history's most hellish nightmare. I cannot help but wonder if there is some sort of mental cut-off, a type of defence mechanism, that the mind puts up to protect one's sanity against the ultimate horror of trying to survive trench warfare. If so, it seems to have protected Charles well enough. Today he appears to be an easy going friendly man who takes life a day at a time and gets pleasure out of small things. Yet this is a man who has experienced the extremes of human suffering, misery and hardship.

He appeared slightly reluctant to discuss his private life, so I did not press him for details. He was born and brought up in Sutton in South London and still lives in that area. He started his working life in the heavy engineering trade and, after the war, got married and went back to the same type of work.

What is more, he stayed with the same company for over forty-five years and by all accounts was liked and respected by all who worked with him.

He kindly gave me an audio tape that he recorded back in 1984 in which he talks about the war and his life.

"I wanted to put my experiences of fourteen-eighteen on record before I got old and my memory failed me", he said, but today, almost ten years later, his memory of those eventful days was a sharp as ever. The tape was a help in checking times and places but in a face to face conversation we were able to cover much more detail.

He told me how in 1991 he visited Belgium on Armistice Day with the Western Front Association and during the tour of the Somme battlefield Charles took the microphone to described to the various groups of tourists also on the tour what it was like there in 1916. It must have given the scene extra interest to have a guide who was actually there some seventy-five years before.

Question: "So Charles, how did you get into the war back in 1914?"

Answer: "Well, all my pals went off to war as soon as it started, so I put a year or two on my age and went to the recruiting office at Croydon, but the blighters turned me down, said I was unfit and said I was blind as a bat in me left eye. And could see 'so-and-so', all on my left side."

Q: "Was that true, were you blind in one eye?"

A: "Well, almost blind on one side, yes, but I could manage O.K, I was used to it, made no difference at all".

Q: "For many that would have been a good excuse to keep right out of it all".

A: "Not for me. I wanted to get in and do me bit. So what I did was, I went along on a different day, when there was another doctor. Now, I'd already memorised the letters on the eye test chart so when they covered me good eye I made out I was reading the chart with me blind eye, and, would you believe it, I was passed A1! So I was a soldier in the 10th Btn. Queen's Royal West Surrey Regiment 41st Division, and was sent straight to Chatham barracks in Kent for three months very strict hard training from 5 a.m. to midnight. It was one long round of P.T., route marches, bayonet practice and on the firing range with the '303, and, of course, non-stop 'bull' – we had to clean and polish everything in sight.

Anyway, it was now August 1915 and the battle of Loos was starting. They took hundreds of half trained lads from our barracks for that battle. Only a handful survived it. Then in May 1916 I was told I was off to France as a Lewis Gunner."

Q: "Why did they hold you back in the UK until 1916?"

A: "Well, I think they knew I was under age. When I first got in I was just under 16 and the uniform drowned me. But now I was looking a bit older. So that was it. Mind you, I didn't even know what a Lewis gun was. Anyway, we got twenty-four hours leave and when I got home my old mum was very upset. She had been writing to the army regular, telling them I was under age and that I should be sent home, but they never answered any of her letters.

So within a couple of days I was in France. Then we were taken by train to a place called 'Plug Street Wood'. That turned out to be my first experience of shelling. Non-stop, it was, and the French and Belgian people did not like us 'British

Tommies' one bit. They even took the handles off the water pumps so we couldn't get any water. We even caught Belgian gun batteries shelling us, would you believe!! During a real heavy bombardment some of their heavy guns were trained on our trenches."

Q: "And they were supposed to be on our side!"

A: "Exactly. You know, they even had their women with them and they used to hang out all the washing on the guns. It was only after some time that our people realised that the way the washing was placed was a way of sending signals to the Germans telling them our positions. No wonder the firing was so accurate and knocking hell out of us. But nothing was done about it. Our command told them to put a stop to it – or else, but no further action was taken.

Anyway, a bit after that me and most of the other lads were sent up the line to go in the trenches. First we were put in a support trench, that's the one just behind the front line trench that directly faces the German trenches only a few hundred yards across no-mans land. As soon as we got into our trench the Germans opened up on us with their big guns. We all had to lay flat on the floor of the trench until it eased up. A couple of rifle grenades hit the parapet of our trench and blew inwards, killing and wounding a lot of our lads. But it was so bad in the front line trench that our lads were being slaughtered. Anyway this officer ordered them to fall back to the relative safety of our trenches.

Now, when the shelling stopped for a while some officers from a command post back behind the lines came up to our trench and said they had seen it all through their field-glasses and demanded to know why these men had retreated. Well, the men told them that their officer had ordered them to 'fall back', but the officers would have none of it and all those men were put on a charge and were given what was called 'field punishment'. They were tied to the big wheels of the cannons, but this almost caused a mutiny. Hundreds of men gathered and started walking round and round the cannons where the men were tied."

Q: "What was that for, then Charles?"

A: "Well, to show their support for them, and it started to get real nasty, so the officers backed down and the men were untied. Mind you, some of the officers could be real swines. For example, one night I was on duty with my Lewis gun. I had to move along the trenches and every now and then fire off a burst of bullets into no-mans land just to keep 'old Fritz' on their toes. So there I was peering out into the dark, ready to fire at anything that moved, when suddenly I saw an officer standing on my right. Straight away he started shouting – 'You were asleep, soldier, you were sleeping on duty.'

'I was not, Sir,' I said.

'Yes, you were,' he said, 'and that's an end to it. I'll see you shot for it.'

I thought to myself – this is it, Charlie, end of the war for you my lad. I was scared because I'd heard about a couple of good blokes who had been executed for being asleep on guard duty. Mind you, they'd had no rest, food or sleep for three days, poor devils. But you could end up being shot for next to nothing, as indeed hundreds of men were. What saved me was a major intervened and sort of pulled rank on this nasty lieutenant. So this old major gave me a right telling off (for something I hadn't done mind you!) and my punishment was I had to go round the trenches for the next week picking up every bit of muck, and getting rid of the dead rats.

Mind you, those executions were bloody frightful things. I felt sorry for those that were ordered into the firing squad because it affected them for the rest of their lives.

You see, when you were charging across no-mans land towards the Germans, there would be men getting hit by enemy fire and falling dead all around you, with dense smoke everywhere, not to mention the most noise you have ever heard, like men screaming for their mothers as they lay dying, the boom of the heavy guns, the screech of shells over your head. Well, with all this going on you only had to turn around twice and you were lost. You didn't know which way you should be facing. So, many a poor lad shocked and dazed out of his mind started to stumble back towards his own lines. Now, when this happened, they were accused of cowardice and of trying to desert, and that could mean the firing squad. Dreadful, it was. To try and prevent this we used to light a big bonfire behind our lines, so that our men could see it and know the direction they had to come from, a sort of landmark."

Q: "What was the food like during all this fighting?"

A: "We were half starved, surviving on biscuits, bread and tea, and once, maybe twice a week, we'd get some soup. But we used to cover for one of our lot while he went behind the lines, to scrounge some grub from the New Zealand or Aussie lads. They were good boys, usually just bread or jam, but we were grateful for it."

Q: "So that was the battle of Ypres, and that's a town in Belgium, right?"

A: "Yes, but it's right on the French border, and after that battle the town was totally destroyed."

Q: "Were you allowed some rest or leave after that?"

A: "Good heavens, no! The next one was the Somme. Now, for that we had to go to Northern France."

Q: "You must have had to go 'over the top' Charles, can you describe that for me?"

A: "Well, you were all in the trench, ready and waiting with fixed bayonets. Some say the waiting was the worst part. Then the whistle would blow. Then you all had to scramble up the side of the trench and go over the top. The N.C.O.s would be yelling like mad men – 'Come on, over you go, kill the hun.' Sometimes there would be a volley of enemy fire and men would fall back into the trench dead before they'd even got over the top.

The first time you go over it's all a blur. One minute you're standing waiting and shaking like a leaf, the next you're over and running like mad, head on into machine gun fire, with shells screeching and bursting overhead. I set off with me mates all around me and clinging for dear life to me trusty Lewis gun. I can't find the words to describe how bad it was. Two of my best pals were killed before we'd covered fifty yards. I saw one shell burst some way off to one side of me, a big one it was. It blew the men directly beneath it to pieces. There were bits of their bodies hanging on the branches of the trees. Well, tree stumps, I should say. There were no actual trees left. They'd all been blown to bits as well. Even the big deep puddles on the ground were turning red with blood. The medics were giving the wounded morphine. But the vast majority died on the battlefield. And we were not allowed to stop and help wounded men. Our orders were to keep going at all costs. At Ypres we used to try and get in behind a tank for a bit of protection, but I couldn't find any in this battle."

Q: "The casualties must have been frightful?"

A: "Well, even now, when I look back on it, I still can't take in the loss of life. It's said that a million men took part in the battle of the Somme, and in about ten months over four-hundred-thousand, that's nearly half of them, were dead. But they kept on bringing more and still more men out from home, as the battle of the Somme moved into its second year. Most of the younger men had perished. So the men arriving from home looked like old men to me. A large number of them must have been around forty-years old, and a lot more in many cases."

Q: "Did you see, or have to deal with the poison gas that the Germans used?"

A: "Yes, I'll say I did. That was deadly, a lung full of that and you'd know all about it. If you didn't die at once you'd have lung trouble for the rest of your short life. But it wasn't only German gas, ours was just as bad. It would take three of us to carry one cylinder, and we'd put them out in rows facing 'old Fritz' across no-man's land. Then it was turned on and it would come gushing out like white mist. Of course, we had to wear gas masks, and they were as good as useless. I recall my one had 'Made in China' stamped inside it. Anyway, if the wind changed direction, and it often did, the gas would be blown back into our own trenches. Then we'd all lay on the floor to try and avoid it. One of me mates, a London boy he was, got a real lung full and started coughing up blood. Bits of his lungs started coming out of his mouth as he coughed. Died in my arms, he did, poor lad.

I admire you for attempting a book about it, but no words could really describe the horror of those days – the rats, the filth, the mud, cold and non-stop rain. No sleep. No food for days at a time and being under constant enemy fire from shells, machine-gun and rifle, and what we've just been talking about: gas. One day I was in the trench and we'd been under non-stop attack for days. Well, two of the blokes with me shot themselves on purpose to try and get sent home and out of the war."

Q: "How the hell did they do that?"

A: "Well, one lad put a tin of bully beef on a ledge in the trench, then placed his hand behind it and fired his rifle through the tin, thinking, I suppose, that the tin would take the full force of the bullet and he would only get a flesh wound. But he misjudged the power of a shot at such close range and blew three of his fingers off.

The other one said to me 'Chas, I am going home to my wife and kids. I'll be some use to them as a cripple, but none at all dead! I am starving here, and so are they at home, we may as well starve together.' With that he fired a shot through his boot. He doubled up in agony and blood started oozing out of his boot. When the medics got his boot off, two of his toes and a lot of his foot had gone. But this injuring oneself to get out of it was quite common.

Another thing the poor buggers used to do was take a bullet to pieces, then they'd take out the cordite, put it in a fag and smoke it. Now this would make them very ill and affect their hearts."

Q: "Didn't the officers in charge realise what was going on?"

A: "They suspected, of course, but it took some proving and, of course, if a man was wounded, he was of no more use in the war anyway, regardless of how it happened. But on this occasion a sergeant-major came to see what was happening. I told him that a sniper had just caught a couple of our men who had to get up on top of the trench for a minute to move a sandbag. He looked at me a bit sideways, but yelled out for stretcher bearers, and they were carried off."

Q: "Where were you at this time?"

A: "Oh, this was at Passchendaele."

Q: "Is that in France?"

A: "Well, no, it's in Flanders, a small town in West Belgium. If I remember rightly, it was the third battle of Ypres in 1917, and this attack on the German lines cost us two-hundred-and-forty-five thousand lives."

Q: "Is that both British, French and German?"

A: "No, just us, the British forces, about a quarter of a million dead. Can you imagine it?"

Q: "No, I can't. It's unbelievable. You said just now your mate in the trench who shot himself, said that his family at home were starving. Was that so? Were people in Britain going hungry?"

A: "Very definitely. You see, in the 39–45 war you had food rationing. People were issued with ration books. It was, hard, most people were very hungry all the time. I suppose you remember it yourself – as a child. You were allowed one egg per week and a quarter of a pound of tea. Things like fruit and fish were unheard of, and as I say, that was very hard for people.

But in 1914–18 it was much worse. For a start the government did not bring in rationing – why they did not is still a mystery to me, as it was to everyone back in 1914. When I returned after the war relatives told me how bad it had been. You see, us being an island hardly any food could get through, because German U-boats were sinking our food convoys. My family lived on bones from the butcher made into soups. And black bread. And when some food did get delivered to the shops everyone for miles around besieged the place. The queues stretched for miles, and if you were old or infirm you stood no chance. Many, especially children, died of starvation. Food riots were very common. But news like this was kept from us, over in France. We only got to hear about it from men who came back after being on leave. I think that's why leave to 'Blighty' was very rare, and severely restricted.

For a few rich people it wasn't quite so bad. They could pay for food on the black market. The government of the day should have looked after the civilians at home far better than they did. Many a soldier cried when he got home after four years and saw the terrible state his kids were in, after four years of near starvation."

Q: "Going back to Passchendaele, Charles, you got through it all in one piece?"

A: "No, not really, I got wounded when we were advancing on the hun – a bullet knocked my gun out of my hand and another hit me just under the ribs. It was like being kicked by a horse. I went straight down. Couldn't move. I lay against the side of this German machine-gun post and I could feel the bullet sinking deeper into me, so I dug my fingers into the hole and pulled the bullet out. The pain eased a bit after that. I can recall a young German boy, lying near me, who kept crying out for water. He was in a bad way, been shot in the chest. Anyway, I managed to give him a drop out of my flask, then, would you believe it, he reached for his revolver and fired a shot at me. I don't think he could see me clearly so he missed by a mile. Before he could fire again one of our wounded lads fired back and killed him.

Well, me and all the other wounded, hundreds of us, had to wait there in the mud for two days with no food or treatment for our wounds until the bombardment eased up. Then they got us down to the field hospitals, where we were treated as best they could for our wounds."

Q: "Wasn't it back to England after that, Charles?"

A: "No, no, by this time they were so desperate for men if they could patch you up and send you back to the fighting they would. I was six weeks in an Australian army hospital. They treated us Tommies' very well indeed. Then I was sent back to me regiment, even got my old gun back. That was a good weapon the Lewis gun was. You know, sort of ahead of its time, invented by an American, I believe, a very light gun, air cooled. Didn't have much of a range, though."

Q: "Where were you by now...I am losing track of your travels?"

A: "Waterloo where Napoleon had his battle, and from there we went straight into Germany. The Armistice was signed and, God be praised, the war was over. And Germany defeated. What finished them in the end you know was starvation, the troops and the Germans at home were just starving. I was stationed in Cologne. The Germans were friendly enough towards us. They were as glad it was all over as we were. In the streets you could see mothers and daughters standing in the doorways of their houses, calling out to our lads that they would do anything for some food or clothing or soap, and they meant 'anything'. The German civilians were in a desperate state."

Q: "Did you get home soon after November 1918?"

A: "No, because Churchill wanted to keep the army mobilised to fight new wars in Russia and Africa, but men were starting to mutiny. There were riots in the navy at some place in Scotland and in army camps all over the place. Oh, and a huge one in London. Thousands gathered in Whitehall at the War Office to demand their release from the army NOW. After all, they'd been away from their families for four or five years. The government backed down because they knew they were losing control of the country.

I stayed in Germany for a bit longer, but when I did finally get home in late 1919, God, it was good to be back in my dear old London. But heartbreaking to think of the millions who would never come home. And there was massive unemployment. But I got work in the end, and stayed with that company for forty-five years – smashing firm it is. I've been retired twenty-five or more years now, but I got a nice pension, and still get invited to reunion dinners."

Q: "This may sound a daft question, Charles, but what do you feel about World War 1 when you think about it all like you've done this afternoon.?"

A: "What an appalling mass murder it all was. I don't think this country of ours, or come to that the world, ever got over it. It wiped out a generation and millions of people grew into old age, living a sad lonely life, always grieving for people who they lost in the Great War."

As I said goodbye to Charles I knew instinctively that I'd met a gentleman and one of life's great characters. And now, when I read the text of the interview or play the tape, it reminds me of one of the most interesting interviews I've ever done, and a fascinating day.

Memorials

Many War Memorials are dated 1914–1919. This is because, although the fighting stopped on the Western Front with the Armistice of November 1918, British soldiers were still dying in other parts of the world. Not least of these were soldiers with the White Russian Forces, who were fighting the Red Army. Others were dying of disease while awaiting demobilisation. Therefore thousands more were to die up until the official end of the war when Germany signed the 'Treaty of Versailles' on 28th June, 1919.

Richard Beasley

(Age 95)

Richard Beasley, 1993

Early in 1993 a news agency sent me a press-cutting with a picture of a sprightly looking old man receiving a retirement gift from a Salvation Army Officer at a celebration dinner given in his honour. The news item went on to state that the dinner was to thank ninety-five year old Mr. Dick Beasley for his tremendous help over the past twenty-five years as treasurer of a branch of the Salvation Army. It also went on to mention that Dick was wounded in 1916 while serving in the First World War.

Of course, at once I picked up the telephone to call the Head Quarters of the Salvation Army, hopefully to make contact with this ex-soldier. They were very helpful and before too long I was speaking to the man himself on the telephone. He spoke with a bright cheerful voice, giving me a date and time to call, and detailed instructions on how to find him.

So, in a matter of days I was standing on the doorstep of his modern maisonette, complete with my tape recorder, note pads and various items of writing paraphernalia..

The door was opened briskly by a very cheerful looking man who was casually but smartly dressed. He had a thick head of grey hair, a strong face and physique. "Come in, young man, nice to see you", he said, and gave me a firm handshake. I replied that it was many years since I'd been called 'young man'. He laughed and said "Well, you are to me, I'm ninety-five". I told him he could pass for sixty-five. He laughed again. But I meant it, he could easily.

He introduced me to his ninety-two year old wife, then insisted on making tea and sandwiches. We sat enjoying them at a small table placed in a large bay window looking out onto a small, peaceful garden.

"So you want to hear about the Great War, young man, the war to end all wars, as they called it."

"First of all, Dick, I said, tell me about your early days, or is it all too long ago for you to remember clearly?"

"No, not at all," said Dick, surprised at my question, "I can remember it like it was yesterday".

And so the interview began.

Question: "Where were you born, Dick?"

Answer: "Hatton Garden, in the City of London, in 1898 and grew up around that area. There were eight children in our family. My dad worked in the print near Fleet Street. It was real poverty compared with today's standards but I look back on a very happy childhood. I realise now how hard mother and dad worked for us all. It's a great advantage to look back on a happy start in life. London was a peaceful city in those days, all horse traffic. It was the centre of the world and everyone you came into contact with was well mannered and helpful."

Q: "As a child, what did you and your brothers and sisters do for fun?"

A: "Well, we had the whole of London as a playground. We'd all walk for miles along the Thames Embankment. In summertime we would cross Waterloo Bridge and head for the big fair ground up on Blackheath. And, of course, tram rides, you could go all over London for Tuppence. Of course, it was quite safe to go into any area in those days. You couldn't do it now".

Q: "I suppose the war put a stop to it all?"

A: "My word, yes. You see, back then there was no TV nor radio, only newspapers. So the press 'made' public opinion. I recall as early at 1911 they started to whip up hatred for Germany and anything German. There was no cinema of course, so our great delight was when dad took us all to the Music Hall. There was also the straight theatre but that was only for the 'toffs'. But for us working class it had to be the music hall. It was great fun. You've never seen people enjoy themselves so much as they did back in those days. Anyway, with all this anti-German feeling, when war did break out we were all at fever pitch and ready to go. The whole nation was up in arms. Almost over night big posters appeared everywhere – on trams, buses, trains, in shops, on the side of buildings – just everywhere."

Q: "What sort of poster?"

A: "Well, the one with Lord Kitchener pointing at you and saying 'Your Country Needs You'. Another one said 'What would your best girl say if you're not in Khaki?' Then another with a little girl asking 'What did you do in the war, daddy?' It was like a madness, everyone wanted to go off to war. Never dreaming, of course, that for most of them it would be a one-way trip. I tried to join up at once but was turned down because I was too young. But I did get in about a year later in 1915 by lying about my age. The recruiting sergeant knew I was lying, of course, but turned a blind eye like they did for thousands of others. Two lads in my lot were only fourteen – and they looked it. They both got killed later in the war."

Q: "So what age were you when you put on a uniform?"

A: "Just turned seventeen, and they put me in the Kings Royal Rifles. I signed on at Finsbury Barracks and in no time at all I was at the railway station getting on a train for Winchester. All my family came to see me off. It was a very sad time. I recall mother and dad being very upset. We were all in tears. First time that we had ever been parted as a family. And of course people were more emotional, they showed their feelings more openly back in those days. Army life came as a tremendous shock, I can tell you. We soon understood that an officer was equivalent to God! And most of our time was spent learning how to fire a rifle, march in step and wear a uniform correctly. And, of course how to salute an officer. Two weeks later we were taken by lorries to Seaford barracks, near Brighton, for three months hard basic training. And I do mean hard. Part of these barracks were a prison camp for German prisoners who would stand forlornly looking at us through the barbed wire fence around their compound.

The first day we were all assembled on the camp square at about 5 a.m. Our sergeant said 'You see this pack of scum' (pointing at the prisoners), 'well I am here to teach you useless shit how to kill these bastards.' With that he kicked the fence viciously. The prisoners looked petrified. I suppose they thought they were going to be shot! Not speaking English they couldn't understand what the sergeant was saying. Just as well, really. Then he went on – 'And if you don't listen to every word I tell you, or you think you know better than me, then you'll be very sorry in a few weeks' time when you're in the trenches fighting hand to hand for your life, because if you've not paid attention today, then it will be you being killed instead of you doing the killing. Do you all U N D E R S T A N D me?' He yelled at the top of his voice. We were all as terror struck as the Germans, but in one voice we all managed to say 'Yes,

Sergeant, we understand'. But I don't think any of us did. Not in our worst nightmares did we ever come close to realising what was facing us. There's just no words to describe it. I have read many books on World War I, but somehow they fail to tell the absolute evil of it all. Training at Seaford was as hard as it could be, it killed some of the older men. Of course, to me then, old was anyone over thirty-five!"

Q: "Tell me about your training."

A: "Well, we had to march for miles, fifteen miles a day most days. And carry full pack. That's ground sheet, tin, hat, billycan, spare boots, maps, ammo and that heavy clumsy '303 rifle. Then there was hours of bayonet practice. Sand bags were hung up and you had to charge them with fixed bayonets, plunge it into the bag as though you were killing a man, then put your foot against it and pull the bayonet out. Then lunge it in again and again. All this time the N.C.O's were shouting and screaming at you – go on kill the hun, kill him, go on stick it in and make sure 'old Fritz' is a gonner. They were trying to turn us into animals. That's what training is really all about."

Q: "Did you get some leave after your training?"

A: "Not blooming likely. Oh, no, straight off to France, Le Havre, for a week under canvas, cold and wet it was. Then up to the front by lorry, but I recall a hell of a lot of marching too. We were all exhausted. I was not yet eighteen, so it was all a bit of adventure to me. Firing guns, sailing on ships to France, when, up until then, I'd never left London. But the older men really did suffer. Because of such heavy losses, men over forty were being called up. They had wives and big families at home and a lot of these men were in poor health. They just couldn't keep up. Their feet would swell and blister and get infected.

Some were very deaf or wore strong glasses. How could they carry loads through miles of deep mud and sleep in open trenches? One chap we nicknamed 'Dad' because he was above forty fell face down in the mud beside me. When I pulled him up he was dead. He just dropped dead from exhaustion. 'No time to stop' said our sergeant. 'Take his ammo and leave him where he is.' Real nice chap he was too, came from Kent and was always talking about it. But you see, human life had come to mean nothing. In training the food was just about eatable but in France we were starving. All we lived on was tea and dog biscuits. If we got meat once a week we were lucky, but imagine trying to eat, standing in a trench full of water with the smell of dead bodies nearby. Mind you we did look a sight. Our heads had been shaved because of fleas and lice, you see. And I was proud of my good head of hair. Like most young men are I suppose. Of course, if you left your food the rats would soon grab it. Those rats were fearless. Sometimes we'd shoot the filthy swines. But you would be put on a charge, for wasting ammo, if the Sergeant caught you."

Q: "How did you get on with the French?"

A: "Not all that well. They were not all that friendly, I think most of them were pro-German."

Q: "Do you remember what your wages were?"

A: "Yes, I do, one shilling a day (5p), but half was sent home to my mother, so I got three shillings and sixpence (18p) a week.
My first battle was at 'High Wood'. It was horrendous. Many of my pals were killed and so many lost their minds with shell shock. It was non-stop, fierce and bloody fighting for weeks and weeks. Trench illness took an awful toll as well.

Men were put out of action in their hundreds by fever, pleurisy, jaundice and diarrhoea. Their limbs got twisted up with rheumatism because of being in cold water all day. Many were made lame for life because of 'trench foot'. It wasn't unusual to see a man cry all day long because their nerves were smashed – what you'd call today a nervous breakdown. I've seen men go raving mad and shoot themselves. At 'High Wood' we had a few tanks. They were O.K. up to a point, but moved very slowly and the German field gunners were very accurate, often scored a direct hit on them. Those early tanks, their fuels tanks were not well protected and when hit they burst into a sheet of flames. The poor crew were nine times out of ten burnt to death. Our guns pounded the German lines night and day non-stop. The noise was beyond belief. Many gunners became deaf for life afterwards."

Q: "How did you get wounded, Dick?"

A: "Oh, I shouldn't talk about my wounds, not when you remember on one day alone we lost sixty thousand men."

(At this point, Dick looked tired and sad at recalling these events. I offered to return and continue the interview another day, but he would not hear of it and after more tea he insisted we carry on with the interview).

Q: "So you got injured Dick, how did it happen?"

A: "I was on my knees in the trench trying to avoid sniper-fire when heavy shelling started. One landed nearby and blew a group of our lads to bits, heads, legs and arms went in all directions. I was blown up in the air and remember nothing more until I woke hours later. Anyway, stretcher bearers dug me out of the mud. My shoulder, arm and ribs were smashed to bits, and I was carted off to what we called a 'Butchers Shop', that's a field hospital, just a tent in a field just out of German gun range. Well, in those tents the young doctors were cutting off limbs all day long and I was scared of losing my arm. The pain was hellish and I kept passing out.

I was very lucky I kept my arm. They patched me up and sent me home to dear old 'Blighty'. I spent the next eight months in a Military Hospital in Weymouth and lost count of the operations that I had. I was classed as unfit for war service in the summer of 1917."

Q: "Did the injury affect you in later life?"

A: "Well, as you see I can't lift this arm even as high as my shoulder."

(Dick stood up to demonstrate that not only could he not lift the arm but also one arm was at least three inches shorter than the other.)

Q: "What was it like to get back to 'Civvy Street'?"

A: "Well, I soon realised that people at home had been kept in the dark about how the men were suffering over in France. People would shout at you in the street things like 'Get a uniform on, go and fight, you coward'. That used to hurt, I can tell you."

Q: "Was it hard to find work?"

A: "It was. And a terrible 'flu epidemic was sweeping the country. If you got it you were ill for weeks and as weak as a kitten for months afterwards. But I did find work after some time and I got married in 1919. Life was fine until about 1933 when my wounded arm began to fester and swell up full of poison. I got sent to Roehampton Hospital for more operations. I was confined to bed for about twelve weeks, then a couple of years later in 1935 I was back in again but this time they found the cause. A lump of shrapnel the size of an egg, left over from that shell had lodged itself in my rib cage and was poisoning my whole system. So I was glad when they took that out of me."

Q: "And this lady is the one you married in 1919?"

A: "No, I lost my 'girlfriend' as I always called her after forty years of marriage. Saddest time of my life that was. We had one daughter. Then I married again, and after eleven years that dear lady died. Now this lady is my third wife and we have spent the last ten happy years together. I have two grandchildren and two great grandchildren."

Q: "You seem a peaceful, happy man, Dick."

A: "Yes, I am. I had a bit of a setback three years ago. I couldn't keep my food down. The doctors told me it was cancer. So another operation to remove a tumour, but I am OK now, I feel fine, except for bad dreams sometimes. I dream that I am back in World War I and I see the faces of all those mates of mine who never came home."

Q: "What about the 39–45 war, were you involved in that?"

A: "My word, yes. I was on duty in the City, near St. Paul's and the Bank of England. Went all through the Blitz, we did. Fire watching and working alongside the Fire Brigade. I was in charge of about thirty people, we were a great team. We worked so hard, pulling people out of bombed buildings. I saw many a man or woman lie down for a few minutes' rest and never get up again. Died of absolute exhaustion, just like in the trenches twenty years before. You see they had been working for days and nights non-stop, with only cups of tea to keep them going."

Q: "Any advice to give people after such a long and hard life?"

A: "Well, I don't know. I'm a down to earth sort of chap. Keep life simple if you can and try and help people as you go along. And above all, take one day at a time."

Q: "I forgot to ask, are you a member of the Salvation Army? Because it was that picture in the paper that lead to our meeting."

A: "No, I'm not. I just went along to help run this little club, organise outings for people down on their luck – that sort of thing, and I stayed for twenty-five years. I like the Salvation Army, they do a lot of good work, you know. But I've retired from that. I spend at least two hours a day in my small garden. You must have a hobby you enjoy."

As I left he shook my hand warmly.

"Good luck with the book," he said. "I am so glad that at last poor old 'Tommie Atkins' is allowed to have his say, even if it is seventy years too late."

"Dick," I said, "for the truth it's never too late".

"Like they say", he said with a smile, "the pen is mightier than the sword, or in this case I hope, your typewriter is as mighty as those shells, bullets and bayonets!"

'Big Bertha'

The Germans Krupp family of Arms Manufacturers whose munitions factories in Essen are still in production today, found themselves a hundred times more wealthy at the end of the war than they were when it started. During the conflict they produced a supergun which fired shells on Paris from a distance of over seventy miles away killing hundreds of people. It was mounted on railway tracks and after being fired would recoil back along the track for a mile.

At the end of the war they had almost perfected one that, if based on the coast of France, would have been able to shell London twenty-four hours a day.

'Big Bertha' was named after the wife of Gustav Krupp.

Roy Vandervord
(Age 99)

Roy Vandervord (1993)

The first time I saw Roy Vandervord he was being lowered to the ground on an extension ladder from the sixty foot high window of his retirement hotel by the Fire Brigade who were making a training film, and Roy had volunteered to play the part of an injured victim who had to be rescued. As I watched the film being made from the sea front of his holiday town I assumed he was an actor, dressed in velvet jacket, over six feet tall, and with a full head of snow white hair.

When one of the firemen mentioned that the gentleman on the ladder would be celebrating his one hundredth birthday in a few months' time and that he was an old 'sea dog' who spent the First World War as a German prisoner, I started to arrange a meeting with him as soon as he reached the ground! A few days later I was shown into his large room, with its long high windows looking out over the English Channel – very fitting for an old sailor, I thought.

He greeted me warmly with a strong handshake. He explained that his eyesight was not too good, but that he was used to it as it started to deteriorate when he was a youngster of about forty! A nurse brought in some tea and we began our journey back in time.

Question: "Tell me Roy about your life before World War I."

Answer: "I was born in Southend, Essex in 1894. I am of Dutch descent. My ancestors got a charter from Queen Elizabeth I to come to England as merchants and trade between here and Holland. At sixteen years of age I went to sea on one of the old four mast sailing ships as a deck hand. I went all over the world. It was a very hard life and a dangerous one when we had to 'go aloft' – that's climb the rigging to the top of the masts and furl in the sails. You had to hang on like hell, one slip and you'd be gone, lost in the ocean."

Q: "And you were at sea at the outbreak of the war?"

A: "Yes. By that time I was second mate on an English tramp steamer and studying all I could about navigation. I wanted to get my Master's Ticket and command my own ship. Well, on 22nd July 1914 we sailed into Hamburg harbour. We unloaded our cargo, then to our amazement German soldiers ordered us to stay on board. The ship and crew were held prisoner. So were all the other foreign ships, many had women and children on board. Then on August 4th war was declared. We were at once ordered off the ships and marched to the railway station. I remember on the way people spat at us for being English. We were packed into these long dirty cattle trucks. The guards told us we were going to the Swiss border to be released, but through a crack in the side of the carriage I could see the polar star."

Q: "What did that mean then, Roy?"

A: "Well, with my knowledge of navigation I knew we were going away from Switzerland. I did not tell the others. They were all distressed enough. Men, women and children all packed together. No food and drink, nor any means of sanitation. We travelled for over twelve hours like that. I was young and strong, but many of the older people got very ill. At last we arrived at a place called Rhulaben near Berlin. We were taken to what had been up to a few days before a large horse racing track. The horses were just being moved as we arrived. Whole families were shoved into horse boxes no bigger than a garden shed. I was put in a tiny one to myself. There was nowhere to wash and we were fed on scraps. We got no news of the outside world. As time passed I lost track of what day or even month it was."

Q: "How were you treated in general, were you made to work?"

A: "The guards were the scum of the earth. Cowardly bullies. There were some assaults on women prisoners. This caused riots. One guard was murdered and some prisoners badly injured. There were now about four thousand of us. They were finding it hard to control us. Everyday, along with hundreds of other men, I was taken to a site to break up rocks and boulders in a sort of stone quarry. We did plan a mass break out. We could have caused chaos being so near Berlin, but of course we had to remember they had guns, we didn't.

Q: "So that was how it was for over four years?"

A: "No, that situation lasted about a year. Then suddenly the camp commandant and all his men were sent to fight on the Russian front. Not one of them ever came back. Things got better after that. Our food parcels started to reach us from home. Up to then the guards had stolen them. They had a sort of scheme at home where a civilian could adopt a prisoner in Germany and send small parcels of food and clothing. Well, this girl adopted me. She'd send me pullovers to wear in the winter, food like cakes, tea, sugar, salt, etc. that I'd share with my fellow prisoners. Her letters and parcels saved my life really and years later I married her. But more about that later."

Q: "You say things got better after the first year?"

A: "Well, a new man took over as commandant. He was an old German aristocrat, a Count Von Schwerim. He marched into camp one day in full ceremonial dress, a spiked helmet with a plume of feathers and a long sword. I'll always remember that. And instead of being escorted by a troop of soldiers he just had one bodyguard leading his horse. He then climbed up onto a platform and made a speech saying, in broken English, 'Obey the rules and my orders and I'll see that you are treated with respect. You'll be treated better than you have been up to now. If you don't, it will be out of my hands. And most of you will be sent to work in the mines of Eastern Europe.'

Well, of course, we all agreed to go along with him. He was very brave because there must have been about a thousand of us standing around him. Now the new guards were all men in their fifties, ex-policemen most of them, too old to fight in the war. So we started to run the place ourselves. Had our own 'policemen' to keep order, even our own court. Doctors made a small hospital. It became a small town and we gave the Germans no trouble and they gave us none."

Q: "What about the stone quarry. Did you still have to work?"

A: "No, that all stopped. And the count's wife was English, a lovely lady. So anything we needed we dealt with her and she did her best to help us. Now among the prisoners were people from all walks of life. Diplomats, teachers, professors and tradesmen of all descriptions. So they set up classes. You did not have to attend but most of us did. Now I was young so thought I'd spend my captivity learning something. I attended English classes, woodwork and silvercraft. I learnt to make lovely jewellery. So I filled my days with learning and began to enjoy life a little. And that helped me get over my longing for the sea. I hated being a land-locked prisoner. We had no outside world news at all. Totally isolated. We heard rumours that German parachutists had captured London and that America had come into the war on the side of Germany because you know public opinion in the USA was quite pro-German in many cities. It was touch and go what side they took you know but I suppose being an English speaking nation decided it in the end.

The dull routine of prison life got many down, illness and suicide were very common. Towards the end of the fourth year no supplies were getting through to Germany as the war started to go against them. Food got very short, our rations were down to starvation level. Even most of our 'old' German guards were sent away to fight in France. But the country was beaten to its knees, exhausted, finished. Then the Armistice was signed and we were set free, put on trains to anywhere just to get us out of Germany. I ended up in Sweden and with no help from the British Government made my way back to my home in Southend."

Q: "How did things strike you after so long?"

A: "Awful. I realised how poor and under-fed the working people were, living in such rotten conditions, in streets full of tiny back to back houses. TB was rife, thousands were dying of it. I finally got home about four months after peace was declared yet very few soldiers had got back. It took a long long time for them to return to their families. They were kept in uniform because many in the government wanted our army to invade Russia, overthrow the new communist government and put the Tsars family back on the throne. I believe Winston Churchill was behind that plan. You know the British, German and Russian royal families were all related."

Q: "Do you think the people would have stood for another war?"

A: "No, as a nation we were exhausted, riots were breaking out all over the place. Especially in army camps. The men wanted to be released after nearly five years of fighting. I think our government backed down over the Russian thing because it could have caused civil war here."

Q: "Did you find work on your return, Roy?"

A: "I was lucky being able to go back to the Merchant Navy. The Shaw Savil Line gave me a job. But for most poor devils there was mass unemployment. But my mother, God bless her, insisted that I rest for a couple of months so she could build me up. During that time I looked up the girl who had 'adopted' me. I suppose I was already in love with her from her letters over the past four years. But as soon as I saw her I wanted to get married. We started going out together. Nothing fancy, just walks in the park. I had no money for anything else and within a couple of months we got married."

Q: "So your war had a happy ending?"

A: "Well, yes, we had a good marriage. My wife died twelve years ago. We had a son who went to America but he died in his forties and we adopted a daughter. Sadly she is also gone now. I am the last of the family. I've outlived them all."

Q: "What about World War II Roy?"

A: "Throughout the '39–45' war I taught navigation to young pilots in the RAF. I had my Masters Ticket by then, got that in 1931. But my eyesight was getting very bad and of course I had to give up the sea. And after World War II I went into the insurance business. But in the end I had to give up my lovely bungalow with so many memories and come and live here where I can be looked after. I like it here. Everyone is very kind and I am very well treated."

I stayed talking to Roy for another hour or so. He was thrilled to hear his own voice on my tape-recorder. He had a small recorder of his own and I showed him how to record his own voice. This seemed to give him great pleasure. I left him gazing out to sea. His window was slightly open. By the sound of the wind it was blowing up rough for a summer storm and the waves were crashing noisily onto the beach.

"I can't see it", said Roy, "but I can hear it, and to me it's the best sound in the world."

Authors note.

During my long interview with Roy he told me an interesting story that he heard from fellow sailors during his forty years at sea. I was told this same story by Jack Baird and a very elderly lady who does not appear in this book but worked at the War Office in the late 1920s. I let them tell me in their own words, so that I could compare each story. They did vary but only on small details. There is no hard proof and it can only be classed as rumour but it is one that was persistent throughout the 1920s. I repeat it here in a very brief version as it has a certain interest value, regarding the tragic events of 14-18.

At the time of the capture of the Tsar of Russia in early 1918, a face to face meeting was held between the German Kaiser and King George V in Scotland. A German battleship came close to the Aberdeenshire coast escorted by other German war ships. The Royal Navy was there in force. A powerful launch brought a small group of men ashore in great secrecy they were taken to a large house in the grounds of a castle (this could possibly be Balmoral Castle and the Craigowan Lodge in the grounds). The meeting lasted 2 to 3 days and on the last day the party went pheasant shooting. I asked Roy whatever could such a meeting be about? He thought they were deciding whether to save the Tsar or carve up his colossal wealth. He had $200 million invested in US banks and huge sums of cash and jewellery in London and Zurich (the three men were cousins).

The Japanese, who the Russians were terrified of after they wiped out their pacific fleet in the Russo-Japanese War a few years earlier in 1905, offered to land a fighting force and destroy all before them in order to get to the Tsar and bring him to England. The Russians would have very wisely handed him and his family over without a fight. In exchange the Japanese wanted a free hand to attack and take over the eastern half of Russia after the war. It is a fact that the British Government did offer the Tsar asylum, but King George overruled them and turned down the Japanese offer. As a result the Tsar and his family were murdered.

The story goes that after the war two British sailors approached a London Newspaper with the story. You have to remember in this age of instant mass communication that, back then, the press was the only form of media and could decide what the public could or could not know about. The sailors were arrested, faced a court martial and put in a military prison for 8 years. It is also a fact that the Russian Romanov family descendents of the Tsar spent the 1939-45 war years in the secrecy and safety of Craigowan Lodge.

Roy Vandervord taking part in a Fire Service training film

Blinded by gas.

Kaiser Wilhelm 2nd of Germany (on the right)
with Tsar Nickolas 2nd of Russia

Many who were close to him claimed he was mentally unstable, proud and arrogant with a dangerous temper. His cousin the Tsar regarded him as insane, many thought due to being born with a withered left arm 6 inches shorter than his right which caused him great stress and misery, although there was also a history of mental illness in his family. Throughout his life he had a passion bordering on mania for killing animals. Every day he would go hunting in the grounds of his huge estate in Holland where he lived in exile. Over the years he slaughtered thousands of birds and beasts.

Adolf Hitler the German leader during WW2 (1939-45) was a foot soldier in WW1 and was awarded the Iron Cross twice. Hitler hated the Kaiser who he claimed was responsible for Germany's defeat in the 14-18 war. Fearing for his safety when Hitler was about to invade Holland Winston Churchill offered the Kaiser asylum in Britain, but he stayed in Holland and died at his estate there in 1941 age 82.

Brave Warriors

"The men of the British Army surprised us greatly in the war. We knew that as a nation they were among the most unhealthy and underfed in Europe. And that they suffered appalling housing conditions. One wonders what made them go to war. Yet they proved to be brave warriors in battle. The ruling classes of that country were not worthy of such a people."

Dr. Gustav Stresemann Chancellor of Germany 1923

From a British newspaper report dated January 1914

500,000 UK children ill-fed and diseased

One child in 12 at Britain's state elementary schools is suffering from disease or the effects of poor diet, according to a report out today by Sir George Newman, the Chief Schools' Medical Officer. Of six-million school-children, more than half need dental treatment and a third are unhygienically dirty. One child in 10 has serious eye defects, nearly 3 in 100 has tuberculosis, one in 100 has ringworm and one in 10, he says, needs surgery for inflamed t4onsils.

The Reverend James Seignior

(Age 95)

The Rev. James Seignior

The Western Front Association was very helpful to me in the writing of this book. They put me in touch with several men who served in World War I, although, regrettably, most were not suitable as due to their great age their memories had become hazy and unreliable. However, one gem of an old soldier was introduced to me by that Association, the Rev. Seignior, a tall, thin, elegant man with impeccable manners and a melodious voice. When we first started to correspond he lived with his daughter, Janet, in a mobile home on the outskirts of London. He told me later that he enjoyed letter writing and regarded it as a 'lost art'. This became obvious to me in his letters as he covered many aspects of the 14–18 era and, of course, I looked forward very much to meeting him.

First, my own spell in hospital delayed it, then he had a bad fall, damaging a leg, followed by a second fall that put him in hospital. I began to wonder if we would ever meet in person. After leaving hospital he decided to go and live in a retirement home for clergymen and once settled in he invited me to go along for a chat. The Rest Home is a beautiful place, built over one-hundred-years ago, and set deep in the Surrey countryside. When I drove through the gates on a lovely summer's day it reminded me very much of Hampton Court. There were gardeners everywhere, cutting grass and watering the dazzling flower beds.

As I entered his room his greeting was "Hello, my dear brother", and he shook my hand warmly saying, "We meet at last!" His conversation over tea was very interesting and covered a wide range of subjects. I was also slightly surprised at how up-to-date he was with today's events. He was saddened by the fact that his love of letter writing was becoming difficult due to eye trouble. He had had an operation to try and correct it – "But it's not done much good", he said regretfully.

"Tell me," I asked, "how have you kept so fit in general, you appear to be in great shape?"

"Well, I think the answer" (and he laughed) "I was a great one for the outdoors up until I had this fall, I would walk for miles – up hill and down dale. Now I need a walking stick and, at times, that old chair," pointing to a nearby wheelchair.

Question: "Where did you grow up, Sir?"

Answer: "In Enfield. It's a busy London suburb now, but at the turn of the century it was real country. Unmade roads, and only one horse bus a week into Enfield."

Q: "One a week? Do you mean one a day?"

A: "No, from the tiny village where I lived into the small town of Enfield, one horse-bus a week. The pace of life was very slow and gentle."

Q: "Apart from being slow paced, what was life like for you around 1914?"

A: "Well, I am ninety-five now, so I was just about leaving school as the war started, and I tried to enlist as soon as I could – like thousands of youngsters did. In a way we had to, because there was a lot of pressure on us to do so, by the Government and the press and also by other civilians a lot of the time. I was not very strong as a young chap and I was turned down for army service at my first try. At my next try I think they suspected I was under age, but eventually I got into the Royal Flying Corps in 1916."

Q: "I've been told that by this time the British public were in a real fighting mood. Did you find that to be the case?"

A: "Well, yes, by 1914 onwards it was. But not in the years leading up to that time. In fact there was a great movement for peace. I think this was because there had been a lot of reaction against the Boer Wars of 1881 and again from 1899 to 1902 in South Africa. But of course those wars were fought and won by our regular army. Not that I believe anyone is victorious in war. But World War I was very different. It was the first time that civilians had been ordered into the army by law. Conscription was brought in, you see. So going into the army became compulsory. This was because our regular army would have been far too small. The Government wanted millions of men, and very quickly.

In fact the Liberal Government got into power in 1906 by saying "No more war", and they got in with a big majority by making 'Peace' their slogan. But behind the scenes they lost no time in building up our navy and general defences to war readiness. I would say as early as 1910 the propaganda machine was in full swing. There were anti-German stories in the press, and even in our children's' comics. All young lads loved to read comics in my young days. In these stories the Germans were always cast as the enemy and the message was what terrible things they would do if ever they landed on our British soil. So after a few years of this type of thing the feeling for peace began to slip away and the people began to anticipate war. I wonder if at that time the German people were being told what awful people we were?

I know that about two years before the war, our war factories, or what they called ordnance factories, went into full production, working twenty-four hours a day, seven days a week. Many people got work in them and they could earn very good wages for those times, but of course it was hard, dangerous work."

Q: "Where were these factories that you speak of?"

A: "All over the UK. The ones near me that I knew of personally were at Cheshunt, Waltham Abbey – oh, and at Enfield Lock they had a fire at one, aviation fuel caught alight, you could see flames for miles. They made parts for aeroplanes, you see. And Woolwich arsenal. They had a terrible explosion there too, a great many workers were killed. I believe they were making shells at the time."

Q: "What were you, in the R.F.C?"

A: "I was a wireless operator. The artillery fire would be observed by aircraft and the information sent down to us by wireless in the Morse code. My personal work was with the Royal Horse Artillery and I learned to ride. This was a great help when I was commissioned into the Artillery in World War II, but that's another war and another story.

The discipline in World War I was strict. I used to look forward with excitement to the occasional flight. You could see the war-torn country from the air, miles and miles of mud. You see, millions of shells had blown up all the underground rivers so the land was flooded. Men and their horses would sink into the mud and drown. Conditions were bad enough for us, but nothing like as bad as the Infantry had to endure. Even now I find it difficult to talk about."

Q: "I understand. Just tell me anything that comes to mind, maybe something funny or pleasant."

A: "There was nothing pleasant, I'm afraid. The men on both sides suffered hardship in the extreme.

Ah, I've just thought of something pleasant. My one and only leave in all that time. It was only a short one, but an unbelievable joy to me. I came home and my family took me to see a show in London. It was Chew-Chin-Chow, and I can still recall how happy we all were as we strolled down Drury Lane. That lovely day remains vividly in my mind."

Q: "Do you think the cause of the war was the assassination of Archduke Franz Ferdinand and his wife in Bosnia in June 1914, as the history books tell us?"

A: "No, of course not. It led up to it and gave them the excuse they were waiting for, but the leading nations had been getting ready for war since 1910 or even earlier. When I look back over the years and I think carefully about events, then I believe the 14–18 war was the worst thing that ever happened to our civilisation."

Q: "Worse than the 39–45 war, with the atomic bomb?"

A: "Yes, because 1939 would never have happened without 14–18. You see, almost all the evil this century, started with, or can be traced to, the First World War."

Q: "What did you do after World War I?"

A: "Oh, a long story, but I studied hard and became a librarian. I love books and people, so it was a joy to me to bring people to books and books to people."

Q: "Were you involved in the 39–45 war?"

A: "Unfortunately, yes, very much so. In 1940 I was commissioned into the Royal Artillery and had to spend, like millions of others, the next six years in uniform. The first four years I was based in the UK, then when the tide turned against Germany, I found myself once again in France and Germany."

Q: "Tell me, Sir, what did you find so different about the two wars?"

A: "Mobility, I suppose, Terry. For example tanks, armoured cars and aircraft were in profusion, and if anything, a more vicious enemy in World War II. Yet, strangely enough, more gently regarded. The German people suffered greatly in both wars. My job at the latter part of the war, and for a long time after it ended, was trying to repatriate the millions of people who had been taken for forced labour, or had been imprisoned in concentration camps, both the German and the Russian ones. It was heartbreaking work and had a profound effect on me, and on my outlook on life in general."

Q: "Can you enlarge on that?"

A: "Well, my mind began to turn towards Holy Orders."

Q: "You mean all the suffering you had seen made you turn towards religion?"

A: "Yes, but the suffering, as you call it, had all been caused by evil, and I decided to tackle evil at it's source, which is in the hearts and minds of ordinary people. So when I got out of the army I studied hard and became ordained in the Church of England. My wife was working as a nurse in the slums of

London and by now we had three young children. We felt we could form a team in the church and use the only effective power, the power of God. We are, you see, one of the few countries that has a national church. This does not rule out all others, but provides a minimum upon which all of life can be built. Most of us are just poor blunderers with only a glimpse of what man could be you know."

The Rev. J Seignior, commissioned into the
Royal Horse Artillery (1923)

Q: "You say you wanted to tackle evil at its source. Can you tell me more about this?"

A: "Well, after going through two savage wars and serving so many years as a soldier, it became clear to me that the trouble was not economic or racial. It was spiritual. As you will agree, greed and selfishness can be found anywhere and in this life there is a strong force of evil. It may not have horns or a long tail nor carry a pitchfork, but he, she or it, is constantly on the watch to weaken our defences and keep men, women and children, and even to some extent, animals from the love of God and the life that He offers us."

Q: "Your views, Sir, on today's world. How does it differ from almost eighty-years ago?"

A: "My word, you need an entire book just to answer that question alone, but I'll try.

In the earlier part of this century there was a much more friendly feeling for one's fellow man. It was a richer life, but better sportsmanship, more moral culture, and this sustained us all through evil days. The present aim seems to be to provide more money to buy even more rubbish. Also, the hooligans and the vandals have gained a lot of ground due to the authorities turning a blind eye.

But, you know, there are some wonderful people around doing very good work. Look at the work nurses do in hospitals, for example. Yes, there are a lot of good people about..."

Q: "What about life after World War II, Sir?"

A: "Well of course the church was my life. I spent twelve years in Australia in the State of Victoria. My other two children are still living there with their families, so I don't see much of them. But a grandson who is on his way round the world called to see me the other day. That was wonderful."

After some more tea and good conversation it was time to say our goodbyes. As we shook hands he said "Goodbye my dear brother, may God guide and speed you with your book. I wish you well. God bless you."

I told this good man that I wished him the same.

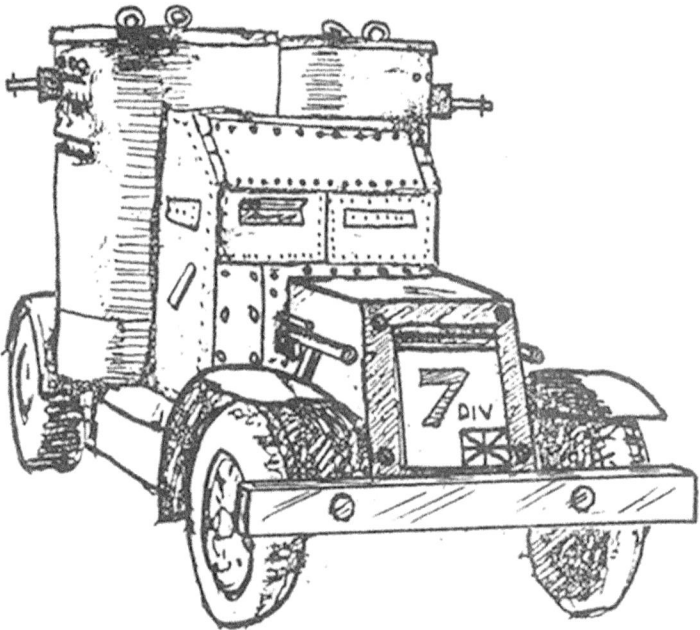

British armoured car with two swivel mounted heavy machine guns at the rear and two fixed, light machine guns at the front.

The Silver Badge

During the war there was a terrible stigma attached to any man not in uniform. They would quite often be attacked and abused in public by fierce over-patriotic women who would give them a white feather – the sign of cowardice. Most of these men, however, had been wounded and, as a result of their wounds, had been discharged from army service as disabled. So to prevent these attacks and to identify these men as disabled ex-servicemen, King George V awarded them the 'King's Silver Badge' which they could wear in their lapel with pride, and it would also keep them safe in public.

'Ecstasy'

The illegal drug ecstasy often used by young people today at wild parties and discos was developed by German doctors around 1912 and used as an appetite suppressant in World War I on front line troops who were suffering the misery of starvation.

Arthur Savage

(Age 92)

Arthur Savage (1993)

This interview proved to be a strange but very entertaining one. A publisher friend who knew I was working on this book sent me a press cutting taken from the latest edition of a provincial newspaper. The headline read ... "Burglar Beaten by Major's Sword". It went on ... "Defiant 92 year old retired army Major Arthur Savage did not flinch when a burglar smashed his way into the bedroom of his home. The First World War veteran seized his ceremonial sword and lunged at the intruder. The startled burglar tried to grab the weapon, but after a short scuffle, decided to beat a hasty retreat nursing a cut cheek and torn T-shirt."

The news story went on to say that the burglar was later caught by the police and was tried for this offence, together with some other crimes he had committed. As a result he went to prison for three years.

It meant travelling some distance, but I knew this Major was too good to miss. I reasoned that any ninety-two-year-old still able to engage in sword fights with burglars was obviously going to be interesting and would almost certainly have a good tale to tell of his army days in World War I.

About a week later, I was walking down the long dismal road in which our Major lived, having got the address from the newspaper. There was no telephone number listed at his address and I got no reply to the letter I had sent him, so it had to be a case of knocking on his door and hoping for the best.

The large old Victorian house lay well back from the road and had long since been turned into several flats. Pushing past some rusting old cars parked in what was once the garden, I rang the Major's bell. The bell was just below a cardboard notice saying 'Arthur, Ground Floor Flat'. As I waited and looked around I noticed the faded curtains and paintwork. It had probably not seen a brush since around 1914! I wondered how an old man of ninety-two lived in such a dump. The words of the burglar in the newspaper story came back to me. At his trial he had said "I only broke in cos I was looking for a place to sleep, I thought it was empty, I never dreamed anyone would be living in there."

My thoughts were brought to a sudden halt by the clanking of a heavy chain being released behind the door. A few seconds later there was Arthur – tall, lean, with a pronounced stoop, but wiry and fit in appearance. Looking me straight in the eye he said, in a gruff voice, "Yes, what's it about?"

I went into my rehearsed speech about writing a book about World War I and, as he was one of the last remaining survivors, would he assist me with an interview? And didn't he get my letter?

"The only letters I get are bills, so I don't bother to open them and I'd love to talk about the Great War. But", he said, leaning towards me in a confiding way, "can you come back in about an hour?" Then he added in a stage whisper, "I have a lady here at the moment."

"Sure", I replied, "I'll be back later", trying not to sound surprised.

"Good man, I'll have a whisky ready for you".

With that the door closed. As I stumbled back down the path my thoughts went into overdrive .. ninety-two-years-old yet still into sword-fighting, hard drinking and womanising! I could be about to interview the nearest approach to Errol Flynn I was ever likely to meet.

I went to a nearby cafe to kill an hour or so, over an almost inedible egg and chips. But my mind wasn't on the food. I wondered if I should wait around outside Arthur's house to see what sort of lady friend he had. Would she be a young raver, or a more mature woman? But no, it wasn't his present that concerned me, but his long distant past that I hoped he could recall.

On my return, Arthur showed me into a poorly furnished little flat and we sat by an old electric fire. He already had a couple of whiskies poured so I switched on my recorder and began the interview. His reminiscences were hard to follow and his train of thought was erratic. His memory for times, dates and places was almost photographic, but at times he seemed unable or unwilling to answer the most straightforward question. For example, he had dotted around the room many photographs of people taken, I would guess, in the 1940's or 50's, but when I asked who they were he dismissed my question with an impatient wave of his arm, saying, "Oh, just family, they're all gone. I've outlived them all. That photo you're looking at is my son, he married an American girl, I went out to live with him for a few years. I like the Yanks, they're a generous, big-hearted nation."

"What part did you live in? Knowing you Arthur it was Hollywood"

He laughed, finished his whisky and said; "No, no, Duluth, Minnesota. But my boy moved on to Canada so I came back here, I missed old England. My boy died out there some years ago."

"I'm sorry to hear that."

"Anyway, I thought you wanted to know about the war?"

"I do, but wars and families are very much connected", I replied. Just then the deafening sound of rock music came blasting through the wall from the adjoining flat. My recorder almost blew a fuse. "Take off your shoe and bang on the wall with it," said Arthur. I did and the volume subsided slightly.

"Don't you find it hard to live here?" I asked.

"After living in the trenches you can live anywhere, mind you we do have rats, but I've not seen any unburied dead lying around." He followed up even a slightly humorous remark with several minutes of laughter.

Question: "How long have you been here, Arthur?"

Answer: "About a year. I came here when I came out of hospital. They said it was temporary until they found me a council place. That lady who was with me, when you called earlier, was a council official who has arranged for me to have what they call Meals on Wheels, so now I'll get a meal everyday, and a house cleaner is going to call twice a week."

He looked pleased at this news. (So my fantasies about Arthur's lady friend were unfounded I was disappointed to learn).

"Do you know, I've been burgled five times since I've been here. I think it's that lot." He pointed with his walking stick at the wall from where the loud music was coming.

Q: "So, Arthur, you were a major in World War I?"

A: "Good God, no, I was poor bloody infantry, a foot soldier in the trenches. I was a 'sit behind a desk' major in the 1939–1945 war, based in Whitehall, I was."

Q: "What sort of memories do you have of 1914–18? Just tell me about anything that comes to mind."

A: "First, we'll have another drink." (He poured two more whiskies). "We had some great men in those days. Great men. We just don't have that calibre of person any more. Of course, we had some real evil bastards, as well."

Q: "Tell me about some of these people you thought so highly of, and why".

A: "Horatio Bottomly, do you know of him?"

Q: "No, but the name rings a bell, wasn't he a politician?"

A: "He was an M.P. but much more as well. He came from poverty, no education, nothing, but he was flamboyant, courageous and brilliant. He became a lawyer and ended up running the Financial Times. Now he was one of the very few men back home who tried to put a stop to the executions of men suffering from shellshock. You see, there was no appeal allowed at their court martial. Bottomly tried to make it so that they could appeal to a court back in Britain and the 'Old Boy' network never forgave him for interfering."

Q: "What was the outcome for this Bottomly?"

A: "He wasn't one of them, so they got him and got him good. He went to prison for seven years for fraud. Something to do with his newspapers going broke. He came out of prison a broken man and died in poverty in 1933.

I was ordered to go on a firing squad once in 1917 to execute one of our own men. It was a hateful job. Every man begged not to have to go on it. I remember the poor chap to this day. He was led out by a military policeman and a priest. He seemed to be staggering, like he was very tired. Then he was tied to this post. An officer went up to put a blindfold over his eyes. But he straightened himself up. He only looked about twenty and wasn't very tall. But I can hear his voice now, as clear as me and you talking in this room. He said 'I need no blindfold. Curse you and your blindfold and may the judges who will surely sentence you one day show you more mercy than you've shown me.'

I admired him for that, and I've never forgotten it. Well then we had to take aim. I couldn't bring myself to shoot him. My hands were shaking so much. So I aimed about a foot to his left. Then we fired. There were nine of us and only one shot caught him in the side. He slumped forward wounded. So I wasn't the only one firing wide deliberately. I thought to myself – oh God no, we're going to have to fire again. But no, this officer, as cool as you like, walked up to him with his revolver and put a bullet in his head. Some of the men were sick, others were crying and cursing the officer who ordered them to do the job.

Now the one who put the bullet in this poor lad's head wasn't one of our lot. He was in the Royal Irish Rifles, name of Colonel Frank Crozier. He was a real evil savage bastard, and he would never miss an execution. In fact he executed one group of men with a Maxim machine gun at close range. He caught some Portuguese soldiers once who had retreated without orders so he machine gunned them, and they were our allies fighting on our side. Talk about blood lust. Those ex-public school officers were all the same type. Crozier had a wife and kids at home but I'll tell you this he used to sleep with his batman, a bloke called Dave Starret and when he died twenty years later he left Dave his entire fortune. Don't just take my word for it, you can double check. When Haig heard about all those murderous executions that Colonel Crozier was carrying out he promoted him to the rank of Brigadier General!

Most of the poor sods were convicted mainly on the evidence of doctors who were officers in the Royal Army Medical Corps (R.A.M.C.) They would not accept that men could reach a point of utter exhaustion when as a result of trench warfare their nerves and brains would snap. These so called 'doctors' would not have it that there was such an illness as shellshock. They insisted the men were cowards and deserters. But I'll tell you this, my lad, no member of the R.A.M.C. was ever put in front of a firing squad."

Q: "All very sad when you expect medical people to protect life."

A: "Well, let's say that those in power in that war had no respect for working-class life."

Q: "So, apart from Bottomly, who else did you admire?"

A: "Oh, so many. Philip Gibbs, later I think he became Sir Philip Gibbs. He was a writer. He went through the entire war as a war correspondent. Wonderful man. He told the truth about the real horror of it all. The dreadful slaughter, the appalling disregard and waste of human life by those in command. But before his reports reached the newspapers back home they were drastically censored. So the folks back home knew next to nothing about the hell that the men were going through. Remember that radio and television were unheard of, even telephones were very rare, in fact you hardly ever saw one."

Q: "So, no one ever read his full reports of what was going on?"

A: "Well, yes they did, because just after the war, I think it was 1920, he wrote a wonderful book called 'Now it can be told.' It was the most authoritative book ever written about World War I. He was alongside the men in the trenches and saw it all at first hand, and he met and got to know all the commanders. He wrote all about them as well. But as you can imagine, no British publisher would dare to touch it. It was unofficially banned. So you know what the man did? He went to America and got it published over there. A few copies found their way back here. I had a copy years ago, must have read it ten times. He wrote other books about the war as well. After the war he did a lot of charity work for ex-soldiers and their families who were suffering, as so many of them were."

Q: "I'll try and trace some of his work. But what of your own personal memories of the war, Arthur?"

A: "My memories." (He spoke slowly and thoughtfully). "They are of sheer terror and the horror of seeing men sobbing because they had 'trench foot' that had turned gangrenous. So they knew they were going to lose a leg. Memories of lice in your clothing driving you crazy. Filth and lack of any privacy. Of huge rats that showed no fear of you as they stole your food rations. And cold deep wet mud everywhere. And, of course, corpses. I'd never seen a dead body before I went to war. But in the trenches the dead are lying all around you. You could be talking to the fellow next to you when suddenly he'd be hit by a sniper and fall dead beside you. And there he'd stay for days."

Arthur fell silent and just gazed into his glass. I decided not to press him on personal reminiscences and just let him talk generally about the war.

Q: "What else comes to mind, Arthur?"

A: "Oh, just the ceaseless slaughter. There was this Chinaman. The non-stop noise of the guns, day after day, drove him and plenty of others completely mad. He went into a screaming fit. The poor soul fell over, went into convulsion and died."

Q: "Surely there were no Chinese involved in that war?"

A: "Good Lord, yes. Britain imported boat-loads of the poor devils, about 70,000, I believe."

Q: "What, as soldiers?"

A: "No, they were used for all sorts of work, cooking mainly. But I saw them burying the dead and any other filthy job going. A couple of them went in front of the firing squad for stealing. How could they defend themselves – they couldn't speak a word of English? I felt sorry for them, and I still do. In 1917 China offered us half-a-million men to fight on the Western front."

Q: "That would have won the war for us."

A: "Well, yes and no. You see, the Allied and German armies were by now exhausted and both nearly beaten to a standstill. They had suffered appalling losses. Now, you imagine bringing in a fresh strong Chinese army half-a-million strong. They would have taken over Europe. They said at the time that America insisted we turn down the Chinese offer. You know, at that time the French had an Empire in parts of Africa and they used to send their black colonial troops in first. They were poorly trained and could not cope with the cold wet weather. We could hear their screams as hundreds of them were cut to pieces by the German shells. Then when the French had the range and location of the German guns they would send in their crack troops.

Another man I recall with great affection was 'Woodbine Willie'."

Q: "He sounds like a Music Hall comedian."

A: "Dear me, no he was a priest. His proper name was the Reverend Studdert Kennedy, an army chaplain he was and he'd come down into the trenches and say prayers with the men, have a 'cuppa' out of a dirty tin mug and tell a joke as good as any of us. He was a chain smoker and always carried a packet of Woodbine cigarettes that he would give out in handfuls to us lads. That's how he got his nickname. At Messines Ridge he ran out into no mans land under murderous German machine-gun fire to tend the wounded and dying. Every man was carrying a gun except him. He carried a wooden cross. He gave comfort to dying Germans as well. He was awarded the Military Cross and he deserved it."

Q: "You actually met him?"

A: "Yes, indeed, he came down the trench one day to cheer us up. Had his bible with him as usual. Well, I'd been there for weeks, unable to write home, of course, and we were going 'over the top' later that day. I asked if he would write to my sweetheart at home, tell her I was still alive and, so far, in one piece. He said he would, so I gave him the address. Well years later, after the war, she showed me the letter he'd sent, very nice it was, saying 'I saw Arthur today, he's very well and will soon be home with you'. A lovely letter. My wife kept it in a drawer until she died.

He worked in the slums of London after the war among the homeless and the unemployed. The name 'Woodbine Willie' was known to everyone in the land in those days. Died quite young, he did, and at his funeral people placed packets of Woodbine cigarettes on his coffin and on his grave as a mark of respect and love. He wrote some marvellous poetry. Have you read any poetry about World War I?"

Q: "Yes. I like the work of Ivor Gurney, Rupert Brook and Seigfried Sassoon. Their poetry caught the moods of the war."

A: "Yes, wonderful stuff, but you must read poems by Wilfred Owen and Edward Thomas."

Arthur then recited some war poetry that he knew by heart. He spoke the words with great feeling and emotion. I found this very moving.

"Of course, what really died in that war was youth, a generation of young men. In my street where I grew up one family lost six sons, all killed in France. The population was out of balance. All through the twenties and thirties a massive surplus of women because so many men had been killed. There were simply thousands of lonely women who grew old alone and never married because they lost their men in the war, and the children who grew up fatherless. The effects were far reaching. So many people were broken and lost for the rest of their lives. Mind you, all the war leaders lived to a ripe old age – except Kitchener, he died in the war, the only one who did, as far as I know. That's why you see, you'll never have a war of that sort again, because in today's wars the leaders could no longer be safe behind the lines while sending men to their deaths a few miles away. Today, if a war started no one would be safe, and they know it. Good thing in a way, I suppose, otherwise we'd have a world war every five years!"

Q: "Tell me about Field Marshall Kitchener. He was the face on the famous poster 'Your Country Needs you' wasn't he? You say he died during the war".

A: "Well, he died in 1916, he was sixty-six, but he died mysteriously. He was the war minister and he mobilised the army. For the first time in England he brought in conscription, he had to – they ran out of volunteers. He started by asking for one hundred thousand volunteers. They were soon killed, so he asked for another one hundred thousand. In the end men were being killed at a faster rate than they were volunteering. So in January 1916 they started compulsory call up. Kitchener was a fierce tough soldier and the regular army was his and they would obey him. The politicians hated and feared him. The government was weak and they knew that Kitchener could take over any time he wished. He had been fighting wars for years in India and South Africa and had the reputation for being ruthless. The press were reporting how demanding Kitchener was becoming, plus we had troubles all over the place. Ireland was on the verge of revolution and in Wales and up north, miners were out of work and their families starving. Strikes – strikes everywhere. So it was a very tricky situation all round. Now, for some strange reason that was never fully explained, the government asked Kitchener to visit Russia as Britain's representative, I think to try and persuade them not to go on to Germany's side. He set off on the cruiser HMS Hampshire and, would you believe, without an escort of any sort. They struck a mine off the coast of Scotland, an area not known as being mined, and there were no survivors. Lost with all hands, it was."

Q: "All very odd, Arthur. Tell me what do you think caused the war?"

A: "I've thought about that many times during my life but I just don't know the answer, but I do know it wasn't the reasons we were told at the time or since. I think it was to do with vast amounts of money, international money. I also know it was planned years before 1914 because I recall as a lad, around 1909, they were always having 'mock' invasions. They would pick a town, usually on the east or south coast of England, and pretend it had been invaded by the German army. Then hundreds of our regular troops would be rushed to that town from camps as far away as the Midlands or London. The military exercise was to recapture the town. This would take a week or so, cause tremendous disruption, then off to another town, and so on."

Arthur Savage (1914)

Picture of "Woodbine Willie"
The Reverend G.A. Studdert-Kennedy. Died 1929 aged 46 years.
He was the Army Chaplain who went with the men into the trenches
heavily armed with a Bible, Wooden Cross, mug of tea and packets of
Woodbines to give away.

Over the top.

The cigarettes that gave The Reverend his nickname.

Q: "What are your memories of your return after the war, the first years of peace?"

A: "Unemployment. No work for anyone. I took a job with a coffin-maker. We were working day and night. 'Flu was sweeping the country. People were dying like flies. They were so weak and under-nourished. They had no defence against illness. You've never seen such poverty as there was in those days. Peoples' living conditions were appalling".

It was getting late. I'd been chatting to this incredible old man for over three hours and he was looking tired. I switched off my recorder and put away my note books. The loud music was still pounding through the wall. I was reluctant to leave him in such surroundings, so it pleased me when he said how much he had enjoyed our journey back to 1914–18. We made some more tea. Then it was time to say our goodbyes.

The next day I got in touch with his local council to see if they could do more for a man of such years, living alone. Within two weeks he was moved to what they called Sheltered Accommodation, where he had his own flatlet and twenty-four hour care on hand. When I telephoned to see if he was all right he told me he was very happy. He even had a television in his room.

"When the weather gets warmer", he said, "do come down. We can sit in the lovely gardens they have here and have a good old chat." I promised him I would, indeed I look forward to it. Conversation and personalities like Arthur's are very rare these days and must be cherished.

"We cannot re-write history – there will be no pardons granted"
John Major, Prime Minister

Early in 1993 Labour M.P. Andrew Mackinlay tabled a House of Commons motion seeking a pardon for over three-hundred British soldiers who were executed by firing squad during the 1914–18 war, saying that many were only teenagers who were shot for desertion and disobedience when, in fact, nearly all of them were suffering from shellshock. They were mostly ill-educated and inarticulate and totally exhausted by the horrors of trench warfare. Also, their defence at their trial (Military Court Martial) was a farce – they were not even allowed to appeal against their sentence.

In February 1993, the Prime Minister, John Major, stated in the House of Commons that after studying all the facts carefully he had decided that history cannot be re-written and that no pardons would be granted.

In reply, Mr. Mackinlay M.P. said that he had received massive support for his campaign and that even if he did not succeed in getting them a pardon they had been vindicated by the most important Court in the land – and that is British Public Opinion.

Was Money The Reason?

In 1924 American newspapers revealed the fact (and this was confirmed many years later by writer Arnold Leese in his book "The Rothchilds") that the powerful international banking family were on very close terms with Asquith, Lloyd George, Kitchener and Haig. Leese states that it was Leopold de Rothschild that arranged for Haig to replace French as Chief of the British Army. Prime Minister Asquith in 1916 secured a war loan with Alfred Rothschild for three-hundred million pounds and credit of another three-hundred million.

Members of the same banking family were friends and financial advisers to the German Kaiser.

Even in the last month of the war Prime Minister Lloyd George negotiated another loan of seven-hundred million pounds because we now had war debts of over seven-thousand one hundred million pounds.

Although unconfirmed, financial experts on Wall Street in New York state that the interest on these loans was so colossal that the British Government had still not repaid the debt by the start of World War II in 1939.

"During the war the international bankers ... swept statesmen, politicians and journalists all to one side and issued their orders with the imperviousness of absolute monarchs, who knew that there was no appeal from their ruthless decrees".

David Lloyd George, Prime Minister
(The New York American. June 1924)

"The World is governed by very different personages from what is imaged by those who are not behind the scenes."

Benjamin Disraeli
British Prime Minister/Statesman & Novelist

Catherine Cathcart-Smith

(Age 104)

Catherine Cathcart-Smith

To meet my lady war veteran my wife and I travelled deep into Sussex and to the elegant and peaceful Rest Home where she has lived these past eleven years. The proprietor was very helpful, but obviously concerned about those in his care, and wondered if my questions would tire or upset her. I promised to bear in mind her great age and frailty.

As we were introduced she put down her copy of the 'Telegraph' saying "I like to read it every day to keep up with world events." She was the eldest of my contacts and I had to approach the interview in as relaxed a manner as possible.

Question: "Can you tell me about your early years, Catherine?"

Answer: "Yes, I was brought up in Chester and my father was a land-owner. There were six children. I was the second eldest."

Q: "Was it a nice childhood, Catherine?"

A: "Oh yes, the world was such a peaceful place before 1914, and England was a lovely country to live in. There were horses everywhere. They pulled all the carts, carriages and buses, you see. Just like you have cars today. You never see one now, except when there is racing on television. Yes, I miss the horses very much."

Q: "How did you learn to drive a car way back in those days?"

A: "A friend taught me to drive on the farm. Father had some of the earliest motorised transport, but it was very easy, you know, because there were no other vehicles on the road. You had the road almost to yourself."

Q: "Lady drivers must have been very rare."

A: "Well, yes, but you know I had a friend who was a dispatch rider and she drove a motor bike during the war. She drove all over the place but I've lost touch with her. She went to live in Australia after the war."

Q: "Tell me about that war, Catherine."

A: "Oh, it was an awful thing. So awful for everybody. I lost my young man, you know. He was killed at Passchendaele. I kept his photo for many many years – until it fell to pieces."

Q: "I'm very sorry to hear that, Catherine. Can you tell me about your ambulance?"

A: "Well, I wanted to do my bit for the war, you see. So I volunteered to drive an ambulance."

Q: "Where did you drive?"

A: "In France, just for a few weeks, but they quickly moved us back to England."

Q: "Where were you driving to and where from?"

A: "We had to meet the troop trains at the big London railway stations – Waterloo and Victoria. I remember the trains had hundreds of wounded soldiers packed on them and we took them from the trains to hospitals all over London. Their wounds were frightful. Young men with no arms or legs. Many had been gassed. Others blinded. It made me grow up very quickly. I had two nurses with me, we made a good team."

Q: "I bet you did. It must have been exhausting work?"

A: "It was, but I kept my ambulance very clean, we had to, you know. And I was supposed to keep the engine maintained, but you know I wasn't very good at that, so the army mechanics did all that for me, wonderful people they were."

Q: "Did you have to work long hours?"

A: "I can't remember, but I think it was ten or twelve hours at a time. I worked at night a lot, because the trains came in all through the night as well. Then I was moved to the south coast to meet the boats as they arrived from France. Hospital Ships they called them. One day I saw this young man on a stretcher and I thought to myself, I know him. Good Lord! It was my brother, so I said to the soldiers who were carrying him 'Put him in my ambulance, I am his sister. They did look surprised. But oh dear he was in a sorry state. Thank heavens my mother and father didn't see him. Our Captain said – 'Catherine, take twenty-four hours off and stay with your brother.' He knew my brother wasn't going to last, you see. So when he died the next day I was with him, holding his hand. I've always been very pleased that I was able to be with him."

Q: "What did you do after the war, Catherine?"

A: "Lots of things. I was a gym teacher for some time."

Q: "That's why you're so fit!"

A: "I suppose so, and during World War II I worked in a bank in London. I was twice Chairwoman of the London Townswomens Guild. I never married, but I travelled a lot and enjoyed life. I was always very active. I came to Sussex to live with my sister, then, when she passed away, I came to live here. The people here are very nice. But I wouldn't like to try and drive an ambulance now."

Q: "You drove it once, Catherine", I said, "and that's all that matters."

The staff were now bringing around some tea and cakes, so we stayed for afternoon tea with this marvellous old lady.

As we left the rest home to start our journey home, what should speed past us but a modern day ambulance with flashing blue lights and siren screaming.

Name Changes

By June 1917 anti-German feeling was so strong in Britain that King George V was advised to change the Royal Family name from 'SAX COBURG-GOTHA' to 'WINDSOR'. The 'BATTENBERG' family also decided to change their name to 'MOUNTBATTEN'.

The Hit Songs of World War I
(The titles speak for themselves)

Keep the Home Fires Burning
Goodbyee, Don't Cryee
Pack up your troubles (in your old kit bag)
It's a long way to Tipperary
Roses of Picardy
Your King and Country want you (and we think you
ought to go)
The Boys of the Old Brigade
The Deathless Army
Boys in Khaki, Boy's in Blue
Just before the Battle
If you were the only girl in the world

Card games.

Albert Church

(Aged 82 in 1980)

Albert Church aged 81

Albert's recollections of World War I make fascinating history, but the way in which I came into possession of them is indeed a strange story. You see, Albert died several years ago and I never had the pleasure of meeting him. So let me explain how I am able to relate to you this man's vivid memories of a time so long ago. It is almost as though Albert knew that at some future date I would be writing down his words, feelings, fears and hopes and that you would be reading them.

There's a restaurant at which I dine regularly and by so doing I have got to know the proprietors quite well, a married couple called Bill and Rita. Rita is the daughter of Albert Church. When talking one day to her I mentioned that I was working on this book and how difficult it was to find men still alive, now getting on for one-hundred-years-old, who could recall and relate clearly their days in the war of 1914–18. Rita looked almost shocked, but then laughed as she said – "My family and I have been waiting about ten years for you to come along, Terry, but somehow I just knew you'd turn up."

Feeling confused but intrigued, I asked her to explain.

"Well, my dear old Dad was a young soldier in World War I and always said that nothing would ever have such a devastating affect on him if he lived to be a thousand. Even as an old man he would get up sometimes in the middle of the night and make a cup of tea, and would explain this by sadly saying he could not sleep – in his dreams he was back in the trenches. Then a couple of years before he died he asked my husband to get him a cassette recorder. Bill got him one and showed him how to operate it. We thought this a bit odd, but just assumed he wanted to record something from his beloved 'wireless'.

The shock came a few weeks after his death in 1983. Among his personal belongings there was this cassette tape, with a letter saying 'Keep and guard this tape for me. At some time in the future someone will come along who will show great interest in it, and, through him thousands of others will learn a little of what my generation lived through, and this may help them to face the troubles of their times. If that person does not appear in your lifetime then please pass it on to my grandchildren, who I know will keep it safely for another generation.

"Well" said Rita quietly, "I didn't know what to make of it all. So I played the tape and must admit I cried nearly all the way through it. A lot of the things Dad talks about I knew nothing of, and I realise now how he must have suffered in that war. To me it sounds as though he's talking to people who are in some future time. He's not talking to his family or his own generation. What ever made him sit down and talk all that into a recorder I just don't know. To me its a mystery, but my family and I are convinced it was you he made it for, knowing that, via you, all that he went through would be read about by people born long after his death."

When I got him home I could not wait to hear what Albert had recorded some ten years before. The first thing to attract my attention was the warm, friendly voice, with its slight Lancashire accent, and I very soon became intrigued by his story of events that took place over seventy-five years ago. Although it was a voice from the grave, it was also being told to me by a man who was there at the time, a man who had lived it, and wanted us to know and share his story. The following is a transcript of that tape recording. The full story is a fascinating insight into life in the early part of this Century.

For reasons of space in this book I have edited out parts that do not directly relate to the war.

One more strange thing about Albert's story is that he recorded it on Armistice Day, 11th November – was that just by chance, with odds against it of 365 to 1? I don't think so.

This, then is Albert's story as he recorded it for us.

"Today is 11th November, 1980. I am 82 years old. I was born in Lancashire in 1898 to a working class family. My father was a clerical man who lived a very good life and had five children. Times were very difficult and money was scarce. I remember Dad paid five shillings (25p) a week rent for the house we lived in, and you could get a lovely piece of beef for Sunday dinner for three shillings (15p). As kids we played in the streets most of the time. Football was our best game. The streets were perfectly safe. There were no strange people about as there are today, and of course, no traffic. No cars. Just deserted except for an occasional horse and cart. But us youngsters, we never caused anyone any trouble. Sabotage – or vandalism as it's called today, was just unheard of..."

Albert goes on to describe his growing up and life in England up to 1914, covering such things as prices of food and clothing, the general mood and outlook of the people of that time. Even his first visit to see a silent film at that most wondrous of places, the cinema, and how, because his family were so poor, he had to leave school at thirteen years and take a 'slave labour' job in a local cotton mill. Also evident in his story is how close he was to his mum and dad and how hard they both tried for him and his brothers and sisters. He also makes interesting comments on the steady rise of the cost of living over that 'Edwardian Era'. His story now reaches 1914.

"When war started I was sixteen. All us youngsters were put in the 'Home Guard' where we were quickly taught to march in step, form ranks and shoot a '303 rifle. They used to tell us that once in the Army 'proper' we would travel to other countries and life would be one long adventure. Well, in those days you hardly ever left the small area around where you lived. For example, I lived about twenty-five miles from the sea, but I'd never set eyes on it, and the thoughts of travelling to other lands was like going to the moon.

So, my pal and I went off to join up. We were so young and didn't know anything and we really thought it was going to be a life of travel and adventure. We'd make lots of pals and have good grub to eat and, of course, not to mention we'd also be getting away from the daily drudgery of life at the mill. My word, were we in for one hell of a shock! Now, although we weren't told it at the time, our dear old country was losing thousands and thousands of men. They were being killed at the front line at the rate of ten thousand a day! So, recruiting was very rapid indeed. At the recruiting depots they were doing all they could to get their hands on anyone who would even remotely pass as a soldier. In fact, in Manchester men and boys were being recruited at the rate of six per minute day and night.

Well, I'd set my heart on going into the Cavalry – don't know why, because I'd never even sat on a horse! Well, at the depot everyone was being put into the Infantry. You've never seen so many men. Queues miles long – talk about 'war fever'. The sergeant said – 'Sign there, you, my lad – Infantry' I said 'No thanks. I don't want to walk, I want to ride.' 'You'll go where you're told', he said. So I went to walk away. 'Come you back here', he yelled out. 'You can go into the Royal Regiment of Artillery'. So the very next morning I was off to a camp near Blackpool. I was terrified of telling mum and dad what I'd done. I couldn't bear to say goodbye to them. So I got up at dawn, dressed like lighting and slipped out of the house and headed for the railway station. When I was waiting near the station I saw my dear old dad coming down the street. He was looking for me, wondering where I was. He looked so distressed. I ducked out of sight. As he passed I could see he was crying. It's not 'till we get old ourselves that we realise the heartache we cause our parents. When I got on the train I was real scared. I'd never been on a train before. What with that and seeing my dear old dad so upset I had to stick my head out of the window and make out I was admiring the scenery. I didn't want people to see the tears streaming down my face. After all, I was a grown man of sixteen.

The situation at camp was absolute chaos. Hundreds of men all being sent off to different places. Me and a few hundred others were packed into lorries and driven all the way down to Salisbury Plain. God, what a desolate place. It was nearly winter and bitterly cold. We lived in tin huts that had a small stove but we were only allowed a couple of spade fulls of coal per day. That meant a tiny fire for an hour or so at night. Training was very hard and tough. Parades, route marches, bayonet practice, target practice – for twelve to fourteen hours a day.

Then, after six weeks, without any warning one night we were on the lorries again, driven to Southampton where an old ferry boat was waiting to take us to France. Packed on it like sardines we were. None of us had been to sea before and we were all sea-sick. What a dreadful crossing. We had to turn back twice because German U-boats were sighted.

We landed at the dead of night and were taken to a camp at a place called Le Havre. What a camp. Old torn tents and sixteen men to a tent, the temperature well below freezing. Then, two days' march up to the front line to a place called Ypres, a real deathbed of a place. The conditions there were vile, just vile. I'd been brought up poor but always clean, but in this battle area cleanliness counted for nothing. There was no such thing as running water, only shell water – that's rainwater that had filled up to the shell holes. But when the Germans sent over poison-gas it contaminated the water, so if in desperation you drank any you'd break out in huge sores. They used to send us up a water-cart, if we were lucky, once a day. Now, for our group of a dozen men we'd get one bucket full of water and we all used that for washing, so by the time evening came, if you wanted to wash, you had to wipe the scum off the top to get a little clean water.

We all slept on the ground in our uniforms with only a ground-sheet to cover you. And your boots as pillows. Strangely enough, though, we could sleep, but then we were so tired and exhausted that nothing mattered anymore. We used to say in the trenches if only I could lose a leg or an arm and get sent home to 'Blighty'.

Every night hundreds of men would march past our guns going up to the front line. They must have thought to themselves that they would not be coming back, and indeed most of them never did. We'd lose hundreds of men every night. I was often sent up there to do what they called 'fatigue work'. Trenches would cave in under shell-fire and whole crowds of men would get buried alive, and we had to dig the bodies out when there was a lull in the shelling. Many had been left for days and were frozen solid. God, it was a sordid business I can tell you. But the officers and N.C.0's did not seem to bother anything about it. 'Come on', they used to shout at us, 'drag those men out of there, or what's left of 'em'. But I was only seventeen years of age, and it affected me very much for the rest of my life.

Why were all these men being blown to bits? For what purpose? No-one seemed to know, except that it was for 'King and Country'. Well, it got round to June or July 1916, the Battle of the Somme was about to start.

Now, about three days before it started, I was fortunate enough to get wounded. It sounds odd to say it like that, but it was fate. You see, I'd been up the line the night before, digging a trench for a cable. Therefore, I should not have been going up again the next night, but one of our lads got killed and I had to take his place. I was allowed two hours to get some sleep before setting off. Well, during that sleep I had a vivid dream where I was shot in the back. I suppose I sound daft saying this but I could even feel the pain of the bullet smashing into my back. It was that real. So when I woke up, me and another lad of about my age went down to the field kitchen and the cook gave us a bit of bread and cheese and filled our flasks with water. Then we set off by horse and cart but when we got near to the place an officer ordered us off and told us to go the rest of the way on foot, and the stupid fool made us leave our rifles behind – said they'd get in the way of our digging, and the big shovels we had to carry.

As I was walking along I saw this German machine gun post, or the remains of it. Our boys had blown it up the night before and it was full of dead Germans. Now, to my amazement I realised that I'd seen it before, a few hours ago in my dream.

Eventually, we found the spot where we had to dig this trench for the cable. After we'd been digging away for hours we then had to get up on top and dig in the open. The officer had told us that it was safe as 'old Fritz' had pulled out of that area the night before. As we had no idea where we were we took his word for it. We weren't up in the open for more than three or four minutes when a German machine-gun opened up on us. The first burst raked the ground in front of us. We both dropped like stones flat to the ground. I pressed myself so hard into the mud I remember it getting up my nose and in my mouth. The bullets made a sort of whining sound as they bounced over us. We were both praying aloud. Our lovely safe open trench was only about seven or eight yards away, but it may as well have been seven miles.

My mate called out to me – 'Albert, as soon as they stop firing to re-load, roll like hell into the trench.' But too late. There was that terrifying pain in my back as the bullet smashed into me, exactly as it did in my dream. I could hear people screaming a long way away, then I realised the screams were coming from me and my mate. By now, he'd been hit as well. I don't remember much after that, but somehow we both managed to roll into our trench where we just lay helpless and bleeding in the mud with no one to help us. I could see my poor mate lying there, so still, and covered in blood. I called out to him – 'Come on old son, we've got to move or Jerry will come over to finish us off. He opened his eyes and said 'Let's hope they do it with a single shot, Albert. I don't fancy being bayoneted to death.'

Then my dad was beside me, looking so clean and smart, like he always did. I thought how is it that he doesn't have a bit of mud on him and I am covered in it? I said to him – 'Are the Germans coming over to kill us, Dad?" 'No lad, no', he said gently. "They think they have already killed you. You be a good boy and just hang on. You'll soon be home again, and don't go running off anymore, do you hear?' With that he seemed to just fade away. And so did I, because the next thing was I was coming round after an operation to remove bullets from my back and legs. My mate was even more severely wounded, but he survived the war, and died a young man in his mid-twenties as a result of those war wounds.

What seemed like a few days after my operation a doctor came along, took a look at my wounds and my frost-bitten feet and said 'How would you like to go back to England, laddie?' I thought, what a stupid question! 'That I would, sir,' I replied. 'Well, if you can get yourself as far as the stores and get a pair of trousers and a tunic', he said, 'then away you go, but you have to get yourself there, you can't be carried.'

So I grabbed the first soldier to help me down there. They fixed me up with some clothes, tied a big label on me saying who I was, loaded me onto a stretcher, took me to a hospital ship and back to England.

I had to spend a few weeks in hospital in Cambridge, then I got ten days, leave, so I could go home. I'd been away two-and-a-half-years. The first news to greet me was that my dear old dad had died a few weeks ago.

After my all too short leave, I returned to my Regiment, I was too knocked up to be a fighting man anymore, but they sent me back to France as a gunnery instructor. That was 1918, and Germany was almost finished by then. And when the end did come, I was in Mons in Belgium where I got demobbed and sent home for good.

Even now I still ask myself – in God's name what was it all for? So much grief, misery and death. In all my long life no one has ever been able to explain to me why that war started. Who started it, or what it was all for?"

On his return to England Albert endured long spells of unemployment, then joined the Police Force and rose quickly through the ranks. He transferred from Manchester to the South of England and ended his career as a Chief Inspector. After the Police he enjoyed running a pub for some years. He suffered all his life from his war wounds and with foot trouble caused by frostbite in the trenches.

He died peacefully at home in 1983 aged eighty-five years, survived by a wife and daughter who tell me they still love and miss him very much.

Albert Church as a Police Officer in 1940s

Albert Church (seated) and comrade who was wounded with him (1915)

Christmas Day in the Trenches 1914

The news item reproduced below is from a British daily newspaper dated December 25, 1914. "The stern disapproval of the Authorities" that the article mentioned resulted in talk of executions and firing squads. It was later decided, however, to reduce one officer to the lower ranks and the men concerned were punished by extra duties and loss of pay.

Truce in the Trenches shocks generals

Dec.25. In one corner of the Western Front, where the British Tommy in his trench was only a few yards from the Boche in his, the war came to a halt, briefly, on this day of Christ's birth.

A Second Lieutenant of the Royal Field Artillery raised his head above the parapet and was astonished to see British and German soldiers standing in the open and making no attempt to shoot at each other.

The Lieutenant met another officer and together they walked along the line as Germans waved and called out. Speaking in simple French, the Germans, holding out cigars, asked for English jam. The extraordinary incident has been much talked about, despite the authorities' stern disapproval.

Rudyard Kipling has written: "Who dies if England lives?" As the year closes, the magnitude of the sacrifices being demanded begins to emerge. British casualties are 100,000; at Ypres alone, the 7th Division of 12,300 men has been cut to 2,400.

Christmas Day in the Trenches
(Two Years Later)

The news item reproduced below is from a British daily newspaper dated December 25, 1916. The front line changed only a few hundred yards in a time span of over two years for such a staggering loss of life.

The Stalemate in the Trenches

Dec.25. The third Christmas of the war has been the bleakest yet. Two years ago the men of Europe had gone to war cheerily confident of being "home by Christmas". Today there is no such optimism. Neither side achieved the great breakthrough they sought during 1916 – and the cost in lives was immense. At Verdun, unofficial estimates of losses are 700,000 men. Further west, the great British offensive at the Somme proved even bloodier; 650,000 Allied soldiers perished, most of them British, along with 500,000 Germans. In places the front lines were changed by a mile or two, but rarely for long, and never to achieve a significant strategic gain.

The Death of Bill Weston
by the late Laurence Shaw
(Age 96)

This interview is sadly one that was not to be. Let me explain.

I was put in touch with a Mr. Laurence Shaw by the Red Cross with whom he worked for many years on a voluntary basis. We exchanged letters several times. His letters were a mine of information concerning World War I. He served as a private soldier in the infantry and fought on the Somme. He was a Londoner but for the past seventeen years had lived with his married daughter, June, in Cheshire. On the telephone he spoke slowly with a strong, London accent. He told me as many others had, that World War I still depressed him. Life before 1914 and life after 1918 were utterly and totally different. He told how men and women thought differently after that war. "It was as though people like my parents who grew up and had a life prior to 1914 were out of step with the world after 1918. Their views and attitudes were not wanted any more. In fact," he said thoughtfully, "people who were middle aged and elderly at the war's end from then on tended to live in the past. They appeared unable to take in or appreciate how Britain had changed."

He went on to say "I have lots of bits and pieces from the war to show you". I told him I looked forward to our meeting in a week's time.

Alas, fate intervened. A few days later I was taken suddenly ill and rushed into hospital where I was to spend the next few weeks. Then, a couple more weeks at home recuperating and unable to travel. One day, at home, my telephone rang. It was June, his daughter, to say that Laurence had died. He fell and broke a bone. This resulted in pneumonia that proved fatal, but if I wanted to call on them I would be welcome to see her dad's war collection. I said that I would.

After my long journey, I was met by June and her brother, Henry, both around retirement age themselves. At the house I was amazed at the dozens of items that the old soldier had kept all through the years: his metal helmet, cap badge, army pay-book and even a German helmet complete with spike on top and leather chin strap. There were letters from his now long-dead wife, even one telling him that he now had a lovely baby daughter, the same daughter that was handing me the letters.

Henry told me that in World War II his dad was unfit for any type of war service due to his wounds from the 14–18 War. Often during the 1940's air raids his dad would wake up soaking wet with sweat and screaming. His wife would say "It's all right, the air raid's over", but his reply was "I wasn't bothered about the air raid, I was having a nightmare about the last war. I was back in the trenches and Germans had overrun my trench and I was being bayoneted to death."

In later life Laurence got very involved in the preservation of wild life and wrote many short articles on the subject, even had a few published in animal magazines.

"Here's one he did during World War I but this one he always kept private. It was personal", said Henry, handing me a sheaf of ageing papers with a story written in careful long hand. Henry went on "he had a close pal called Billy Weston.

This is dad's account of how Billy got killed going over the top. Dad was in a support trench and was in the next wave to go over. As he passed Billy's body, he stopped and took his pocket book with letters and a photograph of his wife and kids, also his wedding ring. He was taking a hell of a chance because by stopping he presented an easy target for snipers. Anyway, after the war when mum and dad lived in London they called on Billy's wife and gave her the wallet and ring and they all stayed close friends until she died in the blitz of 1942."

While we chatted a young member of the family went down the road to get these much treasured papers photocopied for me. On my train journey back that night. I read the tale of one man's death and was strangely impressed. I decided this story should be read. I have had to severely edit the tale down to a quarter of its original size for reasons of space. It is a sad tale of a simple man trying to survive in a terrifying and hostile environment, physically unfit and too old for the ordeal that he faced, suffering extreme fear and hallucinations, probably due to hunger and thirst.

The reason I wanted it included in this account of World War I is because it is a personal story that has remained unread for decades and deserve its small place in history. Laurence himself was wounded the next day and wrote it while recovering in a field hospital. By hearing this long delayed first-hand account of how Billy died, we will have an insight into how millions of men just like him met their deaths in a hellishly tragic and similar, maybe an almost identical way. This, in turn, will advance by a degree or two our understanding of what it was like to die on the Western Front in World War I whether you were "Tommy Atkins" or "Old Fritz".

This is their story. The story of Billy can be multiplied by ten million. Not only is it their story, but it has at long last been told by those that were there at the time. I am grateful that I was able to give them…

The Final Word.

Billy Weston (left) with Laurence Shaw (1916)

How Billy Died

Only a few weeks ago Billy boy, as we call him, was working as a baker in Bermondsey. Lovely chap he is, very polite and quietly spoken. He told me that on his way home from work he would go right out of his way to avoid a pub at the end of his street because people standing outside were always having arguments. Now he is here, in the middle of the world's biggest argument. Married man he is with four little ones at home. He's shown us the pictures of his wife and kids so many times that we all feel as though we know them. He got called up a bit later than most of us 'cause he's getting on for thirty-nine.

We've had four days now of non-stop shelling from the Hun. Some of our lot have gone over the top already, most of them are now lying dead out there in no-mans land, the wounded are screaming for help, poor devils, but no one can get to them. The German machine gun fire has been going non-stop, they don't ever seem to run out of ammo. Billy can't feel his feet any more, he's been standing in cold trench water for about four days now, it's been raining all day so the trenches are filling up. He's cold, wet and hungry. No grub has reached us for two days. Mentally, he is very confused and disorientated. A lot of the time he speaks to his wife. He was overjoyed to see her when she came strolling along the trench, pretty as a picture in a cool, summer dress, white it was with a blue belt. Billy spilled out a torrent of excitable questions. He wanted news of his daughters, his parents, his little garden, was she getting his letters and most important of all, how the hell did she get here? She smiled at him wistfully, but made no reply. Just then Sergeant Judd came along the trench. A regular he is, been in the army all his life.

"Stand by to go over the top", he shouted in his gruff voice. "Right lads, let's give old Fritz some cold steel. Fix bayonets."

Billy tried to slot the long bayonet blade into the end of his heavy cumbersome rifle but his hands were freezing cold and trembled so much that the bayonet dropped into the water.

"Cor blimey, come 'ere lad", said Sergeant Judd to Billy, even though he was about ten years younger than Billy, "I'll fix it for you and if you run out of ammo we'll hit the bastards with these." With that he clipped a couple of stick grenades to Billy's belt and several to his own. "The things I do for you blighters. Do you realise I am disobeying orders by letting you have fully loaded rifles?" he said in a mock whisper. "Major Wordsley said we are to go in with fixed bayonets but no ammo, that way we will be forced into hand to hand combat, but let's say that order has slipped my mind."

"Good old Sarge", called out one of the men. "Anyway, he is so far back he won't be able to make out who's Bosch and who's us."

"What about my wife, Sarge", asks Billy, "Can she stay here until we get back?"

Some of the men, on hearing this question gave a weak laugh. Sergeant Judd was by now no stranger to men of his platoon losing their minds. So he replied quietly "There's no wife here, laddie, they're all waiting for us back in Blighty. That's where we will all be going soon once we've shown old Fritz who's boss.

Just then a young lieutenant appeared at the end of the trench with a megaphone. Raising it to his mouth he called out "Stand by to go over the top. As soon as you hear the whistle, it's up and over. You'll meet little resistance, the German machine-gunners have fallen back behind the lines to regroup. The trench you are heading for only has a small holding-force. Remember you stop for nothing. Wounded must be left. I don't care if it's your best friend or your brother and when you get to the German lines you take no prisoners. Old Fritz knows that, so when he sees you coming he will start running and won't stop until he gets to Berlin."

The men knew better than to believe that one. Say what you like about the hun, they ain't ones for deserting their posts. Far more likely, in fact, to fight to the last man. We all know only too well that Fritz believes in his cause all right. The last hun machine gun post that I overran the crews were out of ammo and their guns had become so hot they jammed. They just stayed there exhausted and hopeless, too dazed even to raise their hands in surrender, just resigned to being shot and killed as our men rushed by.

The whistle blew shrill and loud. Men with their last ounce of energy started to scramble up the muddy rungs of the ladder. As Billy stumbled and slipped his way to the top of the trench he was in a blind panic, knowing in his heart that he was facing almost certain death. He turned to wave goodbye to his wife but her image was now misty and fading away like cigarette smoke into the dark, wet earth of the trench wall.

He started to run with all the speed he could but his legs had turned to lead and his uniform, pack and rifle felt like a suit of heavy armour. He could see all along the lines hundreds of men all doing the same as him, the winter's sun reflecting on the long spikes of their bayonets.

"Spread out lads" yelled Sergeant Judd, "don't bunch up, keep Corporal Weller and me in sight at all times."

This gallant and hopeless band of men were now getting difficult to see from my support trench, but one of the very few to get back is lying in this field hospital with me and gave me the following eye witness account of how Billy died that day.

"Keep running, lads" yelled the sergeant. "At least its stopped raining. Make for that bunch of trees on the ridge."

Billy was now desperately out of breath, his lungs were on fire, his boots were sinking deeper into the mud with every step. Because of the sweat on his face his helmet kept falling over his eyes. The small group were now within easy range of the German machine gun and rifle fire. The gates of hell confronted them. First the remorseless rat-tat-tat of the machine-guns and the 'crack' of rifle-fire. Murderous shells began bursting all around them. The noise alone was terrifying. Men began falling dead like flies. First Corporal Weller was hit in the chest and face.

"Don't leave me, Sarge" he screamed as he lay paralysed with pain.

"Leave you? You're the best bloody corporal I've ever had. I won't leave you, I'll be back, I promise lad."

With that the sergeant began to scream in rage. "Those stupid bastard officers, they've sent us in against entrenched machine-gun fire, they've done for me and my lads."

Billy, along with about forty other men, most of them by now wounded, were pressing themselves into the ground. "Stay down, boys", he yelled, "keep down and don't lift your heads, we'll make a dash for cover as soon as it's dusk". Billy then knew it was hopeless because it wouldn't be dark for hours. Out in the open like this it was only a matter of time before a bullet hit them.

Suddenly a shell burst nearby, blowing off the sergeant's arm. Drenched with blood and crazy with pain he got to his feet and stumbled towards his own lines, his one arm raised in a clenched fist, swearing and screaming "You bloody murderers, you've sent us to our deaths, you've done for us, you scum."

Back at the lines, a small group of officers were watching this horrendous scene through field-glasses. An elderly colonel calmly said to a junior officer "What the devil's that sergeant doing? He's heading back. Is he retreating? If he is, he'll be damn sorry when he gets back here." The young officer, focusing his glasses more carefully replied "Hard to say, Sir, what he is doing, anyway, we'll never know because he's just been blown to pieces by another shell."

Meanwhile, Billy, his face pressed into the ground and shaking from head to foot with tears blinding his eyes, was praying aloud. Along with bits of the Lord's Prayer he kept repeating "Jesus, make it stop, make it stop".

By now his helmet and rifle were gone. He got to his feet and began to walk towards the German lines, arms outstretched, almost beseechingly, and calling out at the top of his voice "Make it stop. Jesus, make it stop".

Several bullets hit him in the legs and in the body. He did not exactly fall down, he sort of sat down heavily with a bump. He looked stunned and then slowly crossed himself and fell back dead. Billy's prayer had been answered. For him it had now stopped.

Later that evening the casualty figures began arriving at the H.Q. tent.

"Six hundred and eighty-three dead within one hundred yards of leaving the trench", said the captain to the colonel.

"Damn shame" replied the old man, "the total for the day will be well over two thousand."

"I suppose so", said the captain.

"Of course, there was no hope of gaining any ground", said the colonel, matter of factly, "but it was a worthwhile exercise to keep old Fritz in his place. Let him know we're here, what?"

"Oh, rather, sir", replied all the other officers in agreement.

In June 1919 at The Palace of Versailles near Paris the Germans very reluctantly signed a peace treaty with the Allied Powers, after refusing to do so for over two months, and then only after the threat of total occupation by Britain and France. They were ordered to hand over territory of ninety square kilometres with a population of seven million people. This area was to be handed over to neighbouring nations. The Allies also demanded the handing over of all armaments including tanks, guns, 'planes, vehicles, shipping, etc., plus an immediate payment of twenty billion marks in gold to be paid into Swiss banks. The left bank of the Rhine was to stay under Allied occupation for the next fifteen years. The German leaders claimed that these were the most savage of terms, especially, they said, as they had not caused the war.

British Prime Minister, Lloyd George, who was present at the signing, said we had been so harsh with our revenge on Germany that he feared we shall have to fight another war all over again in twenty-five years' time – at three times the cost.

Note: Lloyd George was, unknowingly, being optimistic. The second world war started in September 1939, only twenty-one years later.

Jack Baird

(Age 100)

Jack Baird

Pure Evil

Over the years I've thought a hell of a lot about that war, and I'm sure the cause was a force of pure evil. The politician's, general's, banker's and judiciary showed a vicious hatred for the ordinary people of this country and nothing's changed, we're still being treated with contempt. All this political correctness, spy cameras, thought police, deliberately letting crime run out of control. It's all about keeping us down while they have the best of everything. Now they're getting us ready for the next mass slaughter. While they are safe in their panic rooms. Two world wars fighting for our freedom! We're less free now than ever we were. When I stood in France looking at all those rows of war graves I felt betrayed, heart-broken and ashamed.

Jack Baird

In January 1997 I travelled north to Manchester and then on to the suburb of Stretford to meet another person who could give me a first hand account of taking part in the first world war. My mission was to record his views for all time. I refuse to re write history as writers in the future will surely do. These interviews were recorded on tape at the time and you now read them exactly as they were told to me. For the first and last time the men who were there have had their say. They deserve no less.

I found Jack Baird in a small terraced house where he's lived since 1933. He has lived alone these past ten years since his dear wife died, he tells me with a note of despair in his voice. Jack is almost blind and very deaf but with a mind and memory that's crystal clear. So I start by saying tell me about the war Jack.

Answer: The are no words to describe it lad. It was the most evil thing to befall mankind. I joined up in February 1916 as a private in the Manchester Regiment. Then in November 1917 I got run through with a bayonet at a place called Cambray. Our tanks had smashed through the German barbed wire defences and we were running close in behind one for cover, when about twenty hun rushed us and in a hail of bullets the two lads either side of me got hit, one in the neck – he was dead before he hit the ground; the other one was staggering about with half his face missing, blood everywhere. I was petrified. Then I was face to face with a young teenage Fritz and now it all seemed to be in slow motion. First he fired but there was no shot as he was out of ammo. Then I fired at him but in my panic I missed. The next second he's on me and stabs me with his bayonet. I feel it go right through my side. I can still see his face – there was no hate, just a look of utter fear. I felt no pain but as weak as a baby and fell to the ground helpless. Then an amazing thing happened. He got me by the collar of my tunic and dragged me over to a tree, sat me up against it and put my helmet back on my head.

Question: Why did he do that?

A: He knew that more of our tanks were on the way and they had orders to stop for no one, so I would have been run over and crushed like so many of our lads were, but with my helmet on I'd not be mistaken for a wounded German and shot by mistake. Now a few days later I was laying in a hospital tent when I saw this German lad again. He'd been taken prisoner. I told my captain how he had tried to save me but he said it made no difference. Haig had ordered all prisoners to be shot. Now, as this German lad was lead away, he turned to me and gave me a wave and a smile as if to say thanks for trying to save me. I've carried that smile with me all my life. So all I could do was pray for him and myself because the army doctors told me that I was dying and all the poor lads on both sides, and don't forget the animals – the horses suffered – they were shot, blown to bit's and drowned in the mud just like we were. That Haig was a monster. Hundreds of our men were put in front of a firing squad and Haig had the last word. He could have issued a reprieve but in all the hundreds of executions he never let one off. He always signed the death warrant. Then he would go off to enjoy a well cooked meal while we ate snails of the trees because we were starving. When General Haldane was told this he said, "well snails are considered a delicacy in France"!

Q: You sound as though you had no time for those in command.

A: They were scum, take it from me. Those war leaders at G.H.Q. were evil. Their names are forever imprinted on my brain. Haig, Haldane, Macready, Rawlinson, Allenby, Byng, Harper, Most of them were like Macready who was the son of a famous actor. They killed and crushed the welsh miners and the London dockers who went on strike before the war in about 1911. Then after the war they went to Ireland to crush them because they wanted home rule. This was all on the orders of Winston Churchill who hated the lower classes and wanted war with Germany. D'you know Haig and his fellow officers lived in a huge French Chateau about 18 miles back behind the lines and well out of range of the German guns. He had the finest food and wines sent out from London and he even had the latest Charlie Chaplin films sent out to entertain his guests. The house even had it's own cinema! And he had Irish horses sent over so he and the other bastards could go riding each morning with their pretty boy lancers as outriders. There were photos of Rawlinson holding hands with one of his boyfriends. It was published in the German papers but no paper here would touch it.

Q: They would today Jack.

A: It's as bad today. Look at the rubbish in the papers. You're not told the real news. I'm convinced they got a perverted thrill out of sending thousands of men to their deaths. How else do you explain them doing that knowing it would have no strategic gain for us at all? I think they used that war to cull the population like they do with animals. We were the most ill and undernourished nation in Europe and the poverty and slums were just terrible. So I think the establishment wanted to cut out the dead wood and crush the workers, who, as I've told you, were starting to want a better life. The rulers of Britain and Germany were not only related but hand-in-glove. At the wars end Churchill sent our Coldstream Guards to protect the Kaiser from his own people who wanted to kill him and they put all his treasures and possessions onto a twenty coach train and escorted him into Holland where he lived in splendid exile for the next 25 years. He used to hold hunting parties at his Dutch estate where they would tie a wild Boar to a tree and shoot it to death slowly. A shot in the leg, one in the side, until it bled to death and guess who would be there to enjoy it.? Our King George V. and Earl Haig. And I've seen old silent film of those parties so I know it's true. So it follows that if one has that sort of hatred for animals, they must also have it for their fellow man. You see it in our present royal family. They can't go out and slaughter men anymore so they are forever killing animals and birds.

Q: I can't argue with you Jack, you were there and lived through it all, I didn't. You're fond of animals, do you have a pet?

A: I had a dog. I loved him but being so poor on my pension I couldn't afford him so had to give him away.

Q: Do your wounds still affect you?

A: Oh yes I've had breathing problems all my life. That bayonet busted four of my ribs and collapsed my lung. Then later I lost my voice, struck dumb with shock, couldn't speak for over a year and I shook and trembled for years. My hands still shake to this day. And I was unemployed for ten years after I got home. Now I'm in a new war but in this one I've no comrades to help me (Jack laughed).

Q: I don't get it Jack, explain it to me.

A: Well I've been broken into repeatedly right here where I live by local yobs. In the last attack they smashed down the front door, punched and kicked me, flung me in the kitchen and then stole all they could lay their hands on. The police won't do anything to help and the Daily Mail newspaper came to do a story about it but Trafford Borough Council told me that if I spoke to the press they would stop providing me with meals on wheels. But I did speak to them. No modern day louts are going to drive me out my home and no spiteful social workers are going to tell me how to live. I faced the German army so I can face those little maggots.!!

Q: When you look back on it all with the advantage of hindsight Jack, what do you feel?

A: If the lads I saw killed, could see what it all came to, they'd be glad to be dead. My generation and the next one in the 1939–1945 war were deceived, betrayed, brain washed and slaughtered by the politicians, the military leaders, and international bankers. I just hope that they are suffering in hell. They are if there's any justice. At night I still hear the roar of the guns and the screams of the wounded and the dying.

Q: What you have told me will be reported word for word Jack.

A: God bless you for that. It will be the first time it has been since 1918.

A car horn sounded outside in the dark night, my taxi had arrived to take me to the station. I said goodbye to this frail, brave old man at his street door. That's today's enemy he said. Looking across the dismal street I saw a gang of sullen youths wearing baseball caps, drinking out of bottles, then smashing them in the road. I heard the sound of bolts sliding shut on Jacks door. He was getting ready for another night under siege just as he had done in the trenches over 80 years ago. But this time he is on his own – there are no comrades and no covering fire. The police, local council or the government don't want to know if he gets murdered in his own home tonight. Social Services will put it down to a breakdown in communications and Jack will become just another statistic like the millions who were murdered in the 1914–18 war.

Two machine gunners immune (hopefully) from poison gas
by virtue of their respirators

100 Years and Nothing Changes

With regards to Jack telling how the Kaiser, King George V, and Field Marshal Haig enjoyed killing wild Boar on the Kaiser's estate after WW1. It was reported in the British press in January 2018 that Prince Harry, who had recently become engaged to American actress Meghan Markle, flew to Germany to visit his friend Franz-Albrecht zu Oettingen-Spielberg. Nicknamed the *Boar Terminator*, Prince Harry joined him on his vast estate in Brandenberg. There, he and his friends killed over 15 wild boar that can weigh over 400 pounds plus a large number of other smaller animals; stag, deer, fox etc. A hunting pal said Harry enjoys the whole ritual of the hunt in Germany.

Was it an International cull?

This may seem a rather wild theory but three of the men I interviewed, and two who do not appear in this book, told me it was widely believed at the time. As they were there and went through five years of hell their views are worth far more than ours. They pointed out that the ruling classes of the time; British, German, Russian etc. had a fanatical hatred of some animals. They would slaughter these in vast numbers for no apparent reason. They were not wanted for food, for example. So, as Smiler Lovegrove the first veteran I interviewed said; when the stag, wild Boar or birds were in their rifle sights, the only reason for pulling the trigger was the thrill of killing. Now what happens when you put that mentality in charge of thousands of poor working class men? Back then poor really was poor and many who worked on the land were regarded as peasants. Many who came from the cities worked in factories and lived in slums. They were therefore regarded by the High Command as barely one step up from the animals they enjoyed killing every day on their vast estates.

This could help explain why Haig and so many of the generals on both sides, but especially the British, would send thousands upon thousands of men to certain death on suicidal over the top attacks that gained nothing. This is of course not forgetting the vicious and pointless executions. Let us also remember that in the years leading up to 1914 the masses were showing strong signs of unrest. In the UK riots were breaking out with the Welsh miners, Dockers in London, the unemployed in the North. Ireland was moving towards revolution. The same can be said for Germany and especially Russia. Did the European leaders decide to thin out the troublesome population? Maybe it was a cull that got out of hand but it bore all the hallmarks of a definite European cull. Even today on their estates they are still culling animals with high powered rifles when other humane methods could easily be used. Is it just an excuse for killing that showed itself in the wicked blood lust of WW1?

Fred Lloyd

(Age 104)

Fred Lloyd

A few lines in a national newspaper stated that Fred Lloyd, age 104, had been presented with France's highest military award, the Legion D'Honneur as a result of his war service in France during the 14–18 war. The medal was founded by Napoleon Bonaparte in 1802 and only ever awarded to French citizens until very recently when the French government decided to include a few allied servicemen who saw active service in France. The presentation took place at the Uckfield Civic Centre. There was an honour guard of the British Legion and he was accompanied at the presentation by his 80 year old son, also called Fred.

So in January 2003 I set off in the car for Uckfield, a small town in Sussex, for my last face to face interview with a man who was in the First World war.

Fred greeted me warmly in his small room at the cosy residential home that he had moved into just a few months ago. He was bright and friendly with a great sense of humour.

"I've been looking forward to this", he said handing me a cup of tea. "I love to talk but I don't get much chance because people today won't or can't say more than a couple of words.

Question: Tell me about yourself Fred and the early years of your life.

Answer: I was born here in Uckfield in 1898 and started work as a gardener on the Rocks Estate that was owned by the Streatfield family. They were big landowners. I got called up in 1916 and put in the Royal Artillery and then sent to Portsmouth for hard basic training. I was a fit strong lad and used to heavy outdoor work so I could take it. But most of the other lads came from the slums of London and were in poor shape, ill and undernourished. Within a matter of weeks there was an outbreak of Meningitis. It was dreadful. We were all struck down by it and only two of us survived. The rest died or were discharged as unfit for army service because of the shocking after effects of the illness.

Q: What sort of after effects?

A: Many were blind and nearly all of them had lost their hearing, gone stone deaf for the rest of their lives.

Q: So you got over it OK?

A: Oh no. I spent months in hospital and was in very poor health for many a year. When I was called up they classed me as being in A1 health but after Meningitis they downgraded me to C3. Indirectly maybe it saved my life because I was deemed unfit for the trenches. Even so it was no picnic I can tell you – in fact it was hell on earth. Well then, I was transferred to the Veterinary Corps and sent across to Le Havre in France. I'd never ridden a horse in my life but I had to take replacement horses up to the front line. I'd ride one and lead another five or six.

Q: What did they want the horses for?

A: Almost everything, pulling supplies, food, ammunition, bringing back the dead and wounded and God knows, there were plenty of them. There was hardly any motor transport, animals suffered terribly in that war. I won't say they won the war for us but we would never have won it without them. There were thousands and thousands of the poor beasts.

Q: Where did they all come from?

A: Well now, when the war started the government took every horse from all the farms and stables in the land and just left a couple for breeding. From the estate were I worked they even took a dozen lovely thoroughbred Hunters – they only lasted a matter of days on the front line. At one stage so many of them had been killed that we had to import them from Canada and South America. The vets had to shoot hundreds of them because they'd gone blind.

Q: What caused that, a virus infection?

A: No, the vets put it down to exposure, the bitter cold and non-stop rain, but I dealt with them every day and I'd swear it was the poison gas that us and the Germans were using. I've seen horses so broken with fatigue, blind and deafened by the noise of the guns they'd just give up, lay down and die. The same as many a soldier on both sides did. When it was all over, our government sold what horses were left to the French for horse meat.

Q: Did you have any relatives who were conscripted into the army the same as you were?

A: Yes I certainly did, I came from a big family. Mind you, most people had big families in those days. Five of us brothers were in that war. John was eight years older than me. He survived it even though he got a chunk of shrapnel in his head. Then there was Jim, he joined the regular army at 17 and spent 20 years in India and got through it all, but the other two were not so lucky. Poor old Tom was 32 when he was called up and got put in the East Kent regiment. He went over the top with his mates but a shell hit them and his left arm and leg were blown off. He lived for a few weeks in agony, then died of his wounds. He's buried in the military cemetery in France. Then Bill, only two years older than me, so we were very close. They put him in the Scots Guards – just right for a Sussex lad. I bet he couldn't understand a word they said. He was in the trenches and got frostbite. He was in such awful pain he pulled off his boot and three of his toes came off with it! Anyway, he was patched up and even though he couldn't walk properly they sent him back to the trenches and in August 1918, a couple of months before the end of the war he was killed in action. I like to think or hope that some of his pals buried him properly, or as best they could.

Q: I'm sure they did. You still think of your brothers, Fred?

A: Every day of my life – especially Bill. I bet they'd be proud of me getting this medal. Would you like to see it?

I said I'd be delighted and he took it out from the small cupboard beside his bed. Most medals have a rather dull appearance, but not the Legion d'Honneur. It is a very pretty medal, almost jewellery-like. It is made of white and welsh gold in the colours of green, white and silver on a red ribbon. I asked Fred if I could take a photo of it.

"Sure you can, then I'll pin it on and you can take one of me. And how about some more tea?" he asked the lady who had come to take away our teacups. "And a few biscuits," he added with that infectious laugh. He has that sort of expression where the eyes always seem to be smiling.

Q: Is your wife still alive, Fred?

A: No, my dear Alice died 13 years ago when she was 92. We got married in 1921 so we had 68 wonderful years together.

I miss her very much, but then I'm thankful for all those years we had. Never dwell on what you haven't got, think about all the things you have.

Q: One thing you must have, Fred, is very good health because you don't look a day over 70!

A: Not really. When I was 74 I was told I had prostate cancer and had to have that radio therapy. Took a few years to clear up and now I've got a hernia. But as you see it's hard to kill off an old soldier. (We both had a laugh and finished our tea.)

Q: A personal question, Fred. That scar on your forehead, did you get that in the war?

A: No, going to the betting shop a couple of years ago I fell over in the street. Knocked myself right out for a few hours and got taken into hospital. I was damned annoyed about that because the horse I was going to back won and I would have made over a hundred quid!!

Q: What about today's world, Fred? Any strong views?

A: Yes, vandalism. It's the curse of our times. Every shop round the corner in the high street has had its windows kicked in. In my day it was unheard of. Everything today has to be vandal-proof or it gets smashed to bits. What an insane way to live.

Q: Any final views about the '14-'18 war, Fred?

A: Well, you know they say those millions of men gave their lives for their country, but no matter how much you love your country you don't give your life away do you? No, they had their lives taken away from them. At the end of the war Lloyd George, the Prime Minister, said, "I am going to make this country a land fit for heroes to live in." Well, look around you, it didn't work out like that did it? The tragedy is they could have made it that way if they had really wanted to. No, we were betrayed just like today's people are being betrayed. Still you keep going as best you can, that's all any of us can do. I'll be 105 next month and I'm determined to make it to my birthday, same as I was determined to get through that war and back home again as I did in 1919 after six long years. I still grieve for the millions of poor souls laying dead in the mud who never saw home again.

Fred Lloyds' Legion D'Honneur presented to him for his war service in France during the 14–18 war.

Ireland

In 1998 a 100 ft. high round tower was constructed In the peace park at Messines Ridge in Flanders. The tower symbolises Celtic Ireland and Is to remember all those from the island of Ireland who died in a cruel and savage war that should never have happened. A quarter of a million men from Ireland volunteered for service and 50,000 of them died. 30,000 were Catholic Irish and 20,000 were Protestant Irish. They fought and died as comrades and fellow countrymen.

Field Marshal Sir Douglas Haig

Every position must be held to the last man. There must be no retreating. Our backs are to the wall. We believe in our cause so every one of us must fight to the end. (This was an order he gave to the men in the trenches in April 1917). At the end of the war Haig, who was also known as 'The Butcher of the Somme', was rewarded by the British government by being made an Earl and given a lump sum of £200,000. (Today's value over £10 million). Plus a pension of £100,000 a year for life. A report in the 'Star' newspaper dated Nov 1920 states that there are now over 100,000 limbless ex-service men begging on the streets of London. Those too proud to beg sell matches from a small tray hung from around their necks, while standing in the gutter.

Field Marshal Douglas Haig.

The best field marshal the Germans ever had. A self righteous, arrogant bastard, the men called him 'The Butcher of the Somme'. He came from a wealthy background and was heir to the Haig whisky company. Hundreds of Tommies were executed under his command for deserting. How the hell could you desert from a trench, climb out, make your way to the nearest railway station and catch a train home via Paris? What bloody nonsense. They were put in front of a firing squad as a warning to all the other men. That war was the work of pure evil on all sides. I think during those years from '14 to '18 the whole world was engulfed in an evil that has carried on to the present day.

Jack Baird.

He had a great plan of attack. He and his high command sent in wave after wave of men over the top head on into German machine gun fire, hoping the Germans would eventually run out of ammo. The tragedy was they never did, but we ran out of men.

'Smiler' Lovegrove.

Total dead 10 million

When the war came to an end cities and economies across Europe lay in ruins and every family had been affected and would remain so for the rest of their lives. The generally accepted figure for those killed in action is at least ten million. This does not include civilians, those who died of starvation or disease nor prisoners who died in captivity. The figures below were issued by the British War Office and are considered to be very conservative estimates. Many authorities, including those of Russia and Germany, claim the true figure is far higher.

The figures below are rounded up to the nearest thousand.

Great Britain	1,200,000
Germany	2,000,000
Russia	1,800,000
France	1,400,000
Austria-Hungary	1,200,000
Italy	480,000
Turkey	390,000
USA	120,000
British Empire, South Africa, India, Australia, Africa, New Zealand, Canada, etc.	300,000

Further Casualty Figures

Just a very few of the horrendous casualty figures chosen at random with figures rounded up to nearest 1,000. Casualty refers to individuals killed or very badly wounded:

1st July 1916 - 60,000 British soldiers in one day.

June 1916 - Austro-Hungarian 280,000 in one week.

August 1914 – 211,000 French soldiers in two weeks.

April-May 1918 - 350,000 Germans in six weeks.

In the year 1915 - 2 million Russians.

The Author's Family Album

An old scratched and worn photo from the author's
family album (taken in 1915)

My Grandfather, Ted Larsson, died in 1933 aged 52. He was idolised by his children (my Mother, Aunts and Uncles). He worked as a tailor; a gentle occupation in London's West End. He was called up at the age of 40 when he had a wife and four kids at home. In the photo above he is seated on the extreme right, with his brothers. His sad expression says it all. He is pictured in the uniform of the Royal Flying Corps. Due to the massive losses at the front he, along with thousands of others, was quickly transferred to the infantry. He was captured in France while trying to beat off a German attack at Vendueil Fort near St Quentin on the river Somme, and sent to the Stendal POW camp in Prussian Saxony Germany. He was badly treated on a daily basis and almost died of starvation and dysentery.

When he at last got home again he broke down on seeing the state his family were in; a state of near starvation. Unlike WW2 there was no rationing during WW1. He returned, by all accounts, a broken man due to what he had been through in the previous four years. He suffered terrible nightmares and would wake at night screaming in terror remembering the sights he had seen during the war. One of them was when he and his comrades were retreating; they had to run for their lives across a field about 400 yards wide. He told my Grandmother his feet never touched the grass as he ran over dead bodies all the way. Before the war he was a church going man. After the war he said; I don't believe in anything anymore. In one letter he sent home he says: 'All my chums I started off with in the RFC have now been killed, I can't believe I have lived through it all'. He would annoy my Grandmother by constantly saying: 'Mark my words in twenty years time they will take my two boys for the next war. We never beat the Germans they only stopped because they were starving'. He never lived to see it but he was right, my two Uncles were called up for war service in 1939.

The other men in the photo. The soldier on the left, Otto, never returned. Moving forward at night wearing full pack with ammo and carrying a heavy rifle he stumbled into a deep shell hole full of wet mud. The more he fought to get out the deeper he sank. He begged his comrades to shoot him but they refused and tried desperately to save him but within minutes he sank beneath the surface. Two teenage lads who lied about their age to join the army died the same way that night.

The man in the middle, Peter, got through it but suffered spells of reoccurring shell shock. For over a year on his return he would not venture out in daylight.

The man standing on the left, Harold, got four fingers on his right hand shot off and was discharged unfit for service. Before the war he was a tailor, but could no longer hold a pair of scissors or a needle and spent the rest of his life working as a postman.

The man standing on the right, Laurence, had just turned 51 (the upper age limit) at the start of the war so was exempt. He suffered abuse every day. Women would shout at him to get in the army and fight for king and country then give him a white feather (the sign of cowardice). So, heartbroken, he went to work for the Red Cross to do what he could for the war effort.

BUCKINGHAM PALACE

1918.

The Queen joins me in welcoming you on your release from the miseries & hardships, which you have endured with so much patience & courage.

During these many months of trial, the early rescue of our gallant Officers & Men from the cruelties of their captivity has been uppermost in our thoughts.

We are thankful that this longed for day has arrived, & that back in the old Country you will be able once more to enjoy the happiness of a home & to see good days among those who anxiously look for your return.

George R. I.

A letter from the King.

This letter from King George V was sent out from Buckingham Palace to over 200,000 ex-prisoners on their return from the war. It looked so real many thought the King had written it personally which would have been impossible. It was reproduced using at that time state of the art Lithography. The R I after the Kings signature stands for Rex Imperator (King Emperor).

179

A photo with thousands more just like it.

I publish this photo to make an interesting but tragic point. They say a picture speaks a thousand words. The man is my Grandfather with his wife and four children. My Mother is the little girl on the left. He carried this photo with him all through the war. Hardly the image of a fit tough young fighting man. It was taken early in 1915 when he was 40. Within months he was called up and in the trenches because the younger volunteer army were being killed at such a horrendous rate the government brought in conscription. So, he spent the next three years until he was 43 as a soldier along with thousands of other older men, many much older than him, with the upper age limit being 51.

If he tried to join today's army he would be told he was 20 years too old. So what sort of hell must it have been for these middle aged and elderly men with young families back home? No wonder thousands upon thousands of them never returned, not killed by bullets, bayonets, shells or gas, but by sheer exhaustion, illness and age.

To conclude my family recollections of WW1, this is a photo of my Grandfather, now back from the war for 3 years. It was taken in a S.E. London park in 1922 with his two young sons. His Granddaughter Marion Ryder (My cousin) wrote the following poem that I feel sums up the courage of the man and millions upon millions like him far better than all the writings by Historians and Generals who never showed much interest in how these men would cope with returning to the working world after four years of hell and horrific memories they would never forget.

Standing tall, erect and dignified,
In a suit much smarter than the norm,
You face the camera with your small sons,
Crisp In their neatly pressed school uniforms.

Your trilby hat and rolled umbrella;
So different from what you then once wore!
The War to End all Wars in which you fought
For peace; was it all worth fighting for?

No signs of the horrors you must have seen
In your serene stance or in your gaze;
Only pride in your two young sons
Captured with you in that summer's haze.

How did you ever learn to cope?
With the screeching shells and thundering guns;
This happy picture in the park
Seems far removed from the angry Huns.

And though I didn't have the chance to know you,
I send my thoughts to you through time and space;
Your courage and your dedication
Time will surely not efface.

Victors are never judged

Why did we go to war?
What were the real reasons that made Britain declare war on Germany?

As we look back on the catastrophe of 1914–18 it stands as one of the world's greatest tragedies and ranks as one of the foremost mass slaughters of human beings in all history. Very few of the mysterious questions surrounding the evil event have been answered during the interceding years. But even when the media of our present day try and deal with the subject the ultimate question – Why did we go to war? – is never asked, and consequently never answered. Old soldiers like Arthur Savage claim in their recorded interviews that it was due to the blood lust of those who led the British Army, known as the 'High Command', who were, according to Arthur, homosexual ex-public school boys with strong links to the aristocracy. I would not argue with someone who was there and lived through the horror of it all.

But I think we must look even higher up the chain of command, right to No.10 Downing Street – and the top thirty political leaders of the time. First of all our security was never under any threat. We are an island and as such were totally secure. The Royal Navy ruled the seven seas. If you took every other Navy in the world at that time and made them into one, the Royal Navy would still have been twice the size! And far more heavily armed. Our mercenary leaders would have realised that by staying neutral as many nations did, we could let the European nations destroy each other and we would emerge at the end of Europe's war as the undisputed, wealthiest and most powerful nation on earth; with, not to mention, two million of our people still alive. These facts were pointed out to Prime Minister Herbert Asquith at a crucial meeting in May 1914.

However, a group of important men could foresee the terrible dangers facing the British people. Alas, they were not important enough. One was Edward Marsh. He begged Asquith, who's son Raymond would later be killed in the war, to keep us out of it. He held many high ranking posts in the Government. He was also a great patron of the Arts and friend of poet Rupert Brooke who died in the war. He rightly predicted that this would turn into a war that would involve the entire world. But Marsh and his few friends were up against people of immense international influence like Sir Edward Grey who was the Liberal Foreign Secretary. He was a close friend of President Theodore Roosevelt of the United States, and of international bankers like J.P. Morgan and the Rothschilds. He and most of his fellow politicians had massive financial investments in munition factories in Britain and Europe. He told Asquith at that meeting that "Britain was morally obliged to go to war and we must be seen by the rest of the world to be doing our duty". At the end of the war Treasury Minister, Stanley Baldwin, (who many years later was to become Prime Minister no less than three times) was so ashamed of the £120,000 (in today's 2013 value that is close to £10 million) that his investments had made for him during the war that he gave his ill-gotten gains to charity. A nice gesture but it still only represented a fifth of his total wealth. He called on all politicians of both parties to do the same. Every one of them refused. Sir Edward Grey retired to his ancestral home in Northumberland to write books on wildlife. Shortly before his death at the age of 72 in 1933 he was asked by *The Times* newspaper to give an in-depth interview about what part leaders like him played in the war.

He refused saying:

"Victors are never judged".

THIS WAS THE WAR THAT TOTALLY CHANGED THE WORLD FOREVER.

The people had been failed, deceived and betrayed by their Statesmen, Politicians, Clergy and Generals.

They, along with the Crown Heads of Europe and most importantly of all the International Bankers and Financiers had let loose on the world...

'The Four Horsemen of the Apocalypse'...

WAR, FAMINE PESTILENCE and DEATH.

www.ingramcontent.com/pod-product-compliance
Lightning Source LLC
LaVergne TN
LVHW051516080426
835509LV00017B/2075